"Just as the eighteenth-century economist Adam Smith helped explain how the economy helps distribute the wealth, so did his wife discover how the stock market redistributes this wealth, separating the men from their money, taking from the poor and giving to the rich, and effectively redistributing the wealth of the nation."

'Eve Smith'
WHERE ANGELS FEAR TO TRADE

THE CITADEL PRESS, NEW YORK

Illustrations by Rudi Bass

First Edition
Copyright © 1971 by 'Eve Smith'
Published by Citadel Press, Inc.
A subsidiary of Lyle Stuart, Inc.
222 Park Avenue South, N.Y. 10003
All rights reserved
In Canada: George J. McLeod, Limited
73 Bathurst Street, Toronto 2B, Ontario
Manufactured in the United States of America
by The Colonial Press, Inc.
Library of Congress Catalog Card Number: 79-147826
Designed by Reeva Starkman
ISBN 0-8065-0234-7

Contents

Why Angels Fear to Trade 1
Mr. Adam Smith Comes to Wall Street 7
The Theory of the Redistribution of Wealth 9

I THE REDISTRIBUTORS OF WEALTH 15

1. A Man for All Markets 17
   The Stockbroker 19
2. The Co-Redistributors 29
   The Advisory Services and Security Analysts 31
3. A Friend in Need 47
   Borrowing From a Banker 49

II THE DISTRIBUTEE 55

The Rationale of Irrational Man 57

III THE DISTRIBUTORS 67

Completing the Cycle 69

1. The Secondary Distributor 71
   The Invisible Hand 73
2. The Distributors of Glamor Stocks
   and the Cycle of Love 79
   The Making of a Glamor Stock 81
   The Love Cycle of a Glamor Stock 85
   Love on a Pendulum 89
   Divorce—Wall Street Style 93

CONTENTS

3. The Distributors of New Issues — 97
   "The Midas Touch" — 99
4. The Lonely, Neurotic Distributor — 105
   The Short Seller — 107

IV THE POWER BEHIND WALL STREET — 109

Who Are "They"? — 111
Their Crowd — 113

V ADAM SMITH'S MODEL OF THE SYSTEM — 117

The Distribution Cycle — 119

VI THE LEGACY OF ADAM SMITH — 127

How You May Become a Beneficiary — 129

VII THE FUTURE OF THE MARKET — 135

Can the Cycle End? — 137

Appendix: The Ten Commandments of a Broker — 147

A Dedication to the Impotent Investor

Not every investor can make a million; if he could, he would. Not every stockbroker can make a million; he would if he could. This book is dedicated to the idea that any small investor can start with $423.67 and, through nimble trading, turn it into $22.37 in the stock market.

IN THE PAST FEW YEARS, THE PUBLIC HAS BEEN
DELIGHTED TO FIND THAT

Happiness Is a Stock That Doubles in a Year,

THE RICH HAVE ENJOYED PLAYING

The Money Game,

AND THE POOR WERE RELIEVED TO DISCOVER THAT

Anyone Can Make a Million.

Now, after the 1969-70 market debacle, it is time you learned . . .

Why Angels Fear to Trade

THE STOCK market is a mysterious world of wild bulls and voracious bears, of lowly cats and mad dogs, of dire Cassandras and seductive Jezebels, all swirling along a pulsating ticker tape. Every day ordinary people are bedazzled by blinking ticker symbols and flashing numbers. As if hypnotized, they rush into this strange land where sometimes analysts, brokers and traders fear to tread.

Most find the whirling ticker tape an enigma—so seemingly simple to understand, but so difficult to beat. Accordingly, they seek advice from any available stock-market seer. Unfortunately, each expert offers a different axiom, maxim or theory. And, inevitably, each maxim has its contradictory proverb, every contradiction its own contradiction, and every theory flows contrary to reason.

Let us examine some of Wall Street's past and see whether this market lore is still applicable to the future:

There are almost as many axioms as there are stocks.

"You never go broke taking a profit." This is a favorite of investors when they sell a stock and see it go higher. It is very comforting for a person to repeat it several times as he sees the stock soaring to the moon without him.

"You never get rich unless you hold for the long term," is also widely used and contradicts the previous axiom. Most investors do not realize the frustrations caused by this old broker's tale. The profit on paper can dissolve at any moment, but unless the stock is held for years it is difficult to make a large amount of money. This is what causes severe market breakdowns as many people are continually torn between the fear of the stock dropping if held too long, and of it soaring without them if sold too soon.

Now let us examine a revered adage: "Buy low, sell high."

This does seem like the ideal way to play the market. An investor may simply follow the list of new lows for the day in the *Wall Street Journal*. On a certain day he may buy Brunswick at 63, Universal Match at 53, Thiokol at 43, and Transitron at about 33. Those certainly were the lows for the day, or probably the week, but they all sold under 20 not long after. Today's low is often tomorrow's high. This little adage many now be rephrased, "Buy low now, but you may sell it lower later."

Stock market *laws* are different from axioms and adages —they have to be obeyed, especially the ones set by the Securities Exchange Commission. The best known is the *Law of Supply and Demand*, which everyone accepts as the determinant of stock prices except when stocks go down. At that point the brokers make up some new laws, explanations and stories.

Of course, theories do not have to be obeyed or believed, but are usually avidly followed. One of the most popular is the *Bigger Fool Theory*, which states that a person may buy a stock at any price, provided he can find a bigger fool buyer at still a higher price. Proof of the theory may be found when your best friend calls and tells you about the hot stock he bought last week, how it is on the move, and lets you in on it.

The followers of the Bigger Fool Theory also follow its logical extension, the *Dow Theory*, which long ago set up relationships between the Dow Jones Industrial and Railroad Averages (the latter now called the Transportation Average). Both had to confirm each other to predict market movements. If the Industrials were up ten points, most people were delighted; unfortunately, the stock they owned might be down five points. If the Dow Jones Rails should break down, many investors were concerned over their own stocks—even if they owned airlines.

These market principles have had one effect on the investment community—mass chaos. It is easily understandable why the public is confused by this market lore, for there remain many unanswered questions: Why should stocks go down on good news and go up on bad? Why do people rush in to buy stocks at the highs and sell them at the lows? Why does the public always come back after losing so often? Why should brokers, who often follow their own advice, go broke?

The answers are not easily found, but there are some professional people who seem to know more than they are saying. Have you ever wondered why everyone on Wall Street likes to talk about the market, but no one wants to own any of it—at least not for very long? The underwriters who bring out new issues never want to hold the stock more than several days before reselling it to the public. The go-go mutual funds like to trade in and out every 24 hours. The specialists on the exchanges and the traders who make over-the-counter markets would like to inventory a stock less than an hour, or even a minute. The big-block traders tremble every second they are long. And the stock exchanges refuse to ever own any stock at all.

What do they know that causes this "hot potato" syndrome when touching stocks? They must possess some special knowledge about the market for potatoes that the public is unaware of. The Wall Street pros are not fools; they simply have reason to fear rushing in.

The time-worn adages and axioms carry little weight with the financial establishment. They know there is an explanation for the apparent chaos of the market. It does not surprise them when the public rushes in to buy TWA from Howard Hughes at 86 and sell it out again at 16. Nor is it so strange to see Atlantic Richfield's stock rising when it is drilling for oil and plunging when it makes a great find. With General Motors going on strike, companies reporting lower earnings, and unemployment rising, it appears perfectly normal for stocks to begin to soar.

They know there exists a secret theory dating back several hundred years, which illuminates the market for the pros, but effectively keeps the public in the dark. It has never been written down, but has been carefully transmitted from generation to generation on Wall Street. The entire brokerage community will never even admit the theory exists, for they know that a little learning is a very dangerous thing for their business.

How may we penetrate this tightly guarded secret? If no one will talk, we must go back in time and reconstruct the theory ourselves. For our first clue we must turn to someone who was especially good at theories, the noted eighteenth-century economist, Adam Smith. Although well

The Valley of the Dogs

known for his masterwork, *The Wealth of Nations,* which proved to be the basis for much later economic thinking, Adam was also the first economist to test his theories by actually playing the stock market. Let us examine his experiences and adapt his writings to a modern Wall Street. Let us discard the old bromides and clichés and replace them with new ones. Let us create a new market lore that will explain the mysterious world of the stock market. Perhaps then even angels will condescend to trade there too.

"Of all the market losers, Adam had 'em all."

Eve Smith

Mr. Adam Smith Comes to Wall Street

ABOUT THE time the buttonwood tree was being planted on Wall Street in the late eighteenth century, Adam Smith, the first great economist, was busy in Scotland, finishing his masterpiece, *The Wealth of Nations.* Adam was greatly concerned with wealth, especially the acquiring of it. He had theories on everything, including the determination of prices, the distribution of income and the accumulation of wealth. There was only one thing he could not explain:

How could he remain so poverty-stricken?

Adam Smith had an extremely logical mind and soon became a professor of logic at Glasgow University. From his ivory tower he figured it would be easy to apply his brilliant reasoning powers to any subject. And if he could get rich at the same time it would be even more reasonable. And so it was that Adam turned his talents to that great exercise in logic—the stock market.

Through deductive reasoning, he concluded that good stocks go up and bad ones go down. Ergo, he bought on "good" news and sold on "bad" news. He waited for the good announcements—stock splits, dividend raises, oil discoveries—and then plunged in. After the bad news—reverse splits, dividend cuts, and dry wells—he plunged out. For some reason his capital, like his stocks, was cleaved, divided and split in two. It was really quite elementary. Starting with his basic premises and extending them to their logical conclusion, he proved beyond all doubt that he was a loser.

It was then, after many losses, that Adam began to use some common sense. He took himself a wife, Eve, who was homely, viperous and rich. She wasn't much to look at, but her money was. With his renewed confidence and her capital he plunged again, having married her for better or for worse, and for good or bad markets.

Unbelievably, he began to lose more and Eve turned into the first market shrew, whining and crying over the morning breakfast table. "Do you have to chase every beauty on the tape?" she would plead. Adam calmly assured her that in the market reason would prevail. When he was almost broke, Eve discovered that of all the market losers, Adam had 'em all.

Where did the great Adam Smith go wrong? He had believed that the logical reasoning of economic theory could be applied to the stock market, that there is some rationale for market behavior. There is, but it is a logic unique to the market itself and 180 degrees removed from everyday life. Eve, broken woman that she was, could see it. Adam Smith had to be stood on his head, his theories turned inside out, and common sense turned into nonsense. Let us reinterpret his theories and bring a more modern Adam Smith to Wall Street.

The Theory of the Redistribution of Wealth

ADAM SMITH is considered the father of economics for his masterful work, *The Wealth of Nations*. From it, the theories of prices, value, and distribution of income have evolved. The basic premise of Adam and the economists who followed him is the concept of "economic man," an abstract creature who is motivated by purely economic gain. Adam Smith is most famous for describing the self-interest of each individual who labors for his personal gain. He is guided by an "invisible hand" which promotes the general welfare of the economy.

"Economic man" is thus a "rational man" who represents how men behave under a given set of circumstances. He is assumed to act reasonably. If there are two products of equal quality, he will buy the one with the cheaper price. If that price rises, he may buy less; and if it should decline, he may buy more. This eagerness to buy or sell is more easily recognized as the *Law of Supply and Demand*.

Now let us reinterpret Adam and bring his concepts up to date for the stock market.

"Rational man," the basis of economics, becomes "irrational man," the fundamental concept of the stock market. Though still motivated by economic gain, the market man consistently acts irrationally. When prices are higher, he is eager to buy more; when they are down he is eager to buy less and sell more. The cheaper stocks are, the less he wants them; the costlier they are, the more he desires them.

"Irrational man" follows these basic laws of behavior:

1) The less he knows or understands about a company's product, the more he is willing to pay for the stock.

2) The vaguer and more unbelievable the earnings estimate, the higher he is willing to reach for the stock.

3) The more commonplace the product becomes, and the more definite and reliable the earnings estimate, the faster he will sell the stock.

Pursuing this logic, many mysterious happenings in the market are more easily understandable. When record earnings are announced, the dividend is raised, and when the stock is split, the price falls. When reports of deficits and dividend cuts are published, the price rises. Therefore, good news is a reason for selling, and bad news is good reason for buying. We may conclude that the stock market has a logic and rationality of its own, which is essentially irrational.

The intermingling of irrational men leads to a meeting of the minds and the setting of prices. This is *Supply and Demand* in action. Stock prices are simply the aggregate thinking of investors, summed up in our first market principle:

Irrational men set irrational prices

To illustrate, let us consider two big market winners of 1969, Natomas and Atlantic Richfield. Both companies are searching for oil on opposite sides of the world—Natomas in the depths of the Java Sea off Indonesia, and Atlantic Richfield on the North slope of Alaska.

When Natomas began drilling its offshore wells, the stock began to rise. As Natomas' drill bore deeper and deeper, the stock rose higher and higher. When the company's president was quoted as saying, "No one at this time can make a responsible estimate of reserves," the stock soared.

Meanwhile, on the slopes of Alaska, Atlantic Richfield and many large oil companies were bidding for Alaskan oil leases. As the day neared for opening the bids, Atlantic's stock steadily rose. The day before the awarding of the leases, the stock ran up sharply. When Alaska proudly announced the awarding of leases, and everyone began to realize what Atlantic had, the stock plunged. It was simply too true to be good.

With this experience in mind, is there hope for the stockholders of Natomas as the drill bores inexorably closer to the discovery of vast fields of oil? Yes, if they have the good fortune to strike a dry hole, which might require some great luck in the depths of the Java Sea.

Taking the premise of "irrational man" and the principle of "irrational prices," we are now ready to formulate a new theory to explain the overall workings of the market.

Adam Smith, in his theory of the distribution of wealth, again provides the key. Later economists expanded his idea of a market system which determines how each economic group receives its share of income in the form of wages, rent, interest, and profit. Here, at last, is the essence of a new, illuminating theory of the market. The *Distribution Theory* of economics yields to the stock market *Theory of the Redistribution of Wealth: Just as Economics Shows How Each Individual Receives His Share of Wealth, So Does the Stock Market Simply Redistribute this Wealth.*

No new wealth is actually created in the market; the existing wealth is simply redistributed. One man's large gain usually results in ten thousand poor souls' huge loss. In the process a few become *nouveau riche*, while thousands become *nouveau poor*. No new money is created in the market. Stock certificates are simply changing hands at varying prices throughout each day. Someone is always trying to foist his shares at higher prices on someone else, who in turn looks for yet another generous soul. In the end many find themselves redistributed at the highs and ride their stocks down, having found no one new to turn on.

Anticipating Keynes, there is a market "mulitplier effect" which states that as stocks double, the investors' demand for stocks quadruples. Their eagerness to buy at continually higher prices inevitably results in a redistribution of the incomes of the many into the wealth of the few. As the market fluctuates in periods of bull and bear markets, two guiding market principles emerge:

*In periods of high prices
big money tends to become bigger.*

and its necessary corollary,

*In periods of low prices
big investors get thinner
and small investors tend to become miniscule.*

The stock market is thus seen ultimately as performing a vital economic function: that of separating men from their money, taking from the poor and giving to the rich, and efficiently redistributing the wealth of the nation.

Here, then, is an original market theory, showing not only how the financiers of the past—the Goulds, Vanderbilts and Rockefellers—accumulated their wealth, but also pointing out who contributed to them. Most market books are only concerned with the winners and how they got that way, but it is important to remember that for every winner there is a loser. And why should such market heroes as Bernard Baruch and Jesse Livermore receive all the praise? For the first time credit will be given to those who made it all possible.

Every conceptual framework has its special terminology. Explicit definitions need to be formulated. The redistribution system utilizes the following terms:

a) the *Distributors of Stocks*, or the small group of insiders who accumulate stocks at low prices in order to resell them at high prices to

b) the *Distributees*, or the large group of outsiders who eagerly receive them in. The process is aided by

c) the *Redistributors of Wealth*, who work outside the system and are the catalyst of the continual market movement.

These three main groups interweave and intertwine to form a "distribution cycle" which flows up and down during bull and bear markets. Each individual may play many roles during his sojourn in the market, sometimes a *distributor*, often a *redistributor*, and many times a *distributee*.

It is important that you discover who and where you are in the cycle. We shall explore the characteristics of each group so that you may easily identify them. In this manner you may learn to become the *beneficiary* of the system rather than the one who always gets distributed.

One

THE REDISTRIBUTORS OF WEALTH

1
A Man for All Markets

"Ours is not a reason why,
Ours is b; to sell or buy."

Credo of a Wall Street Brok r

The Stockbroker

A STOCKBROKER may be thought of in many ways: Some people consider him a marriage broker matching their money with the right stock; while others consider him a part-time divorce judge, judiciously separating them from their money. But he is, in reality, a versatile virtuoso, a meandering middleman, and a man for all seasons, cycles, and markets.

To some he is a psychiatrist. To be able to talk, to discuss things, and loudly vent one's frustrations on some kind soul, fulfills a basic need in many people. Depending on the mood of the market the bill can be cheaper or more expensive than that of a practicing psychiatrist. Investors would prefer, all things considered, that their broker go to the psychiatrist.

To others he is a friend in need. When lonely, they turn to a broker in desperation, and as long as they have money to swing with, they have found their first true friend for life.

Some people regard brokers as prophets or market seers, and, in all fairness, they should be highly respected for attempting to forecast the future. What other profession is asked every day to try to tell you what will happen the next day? Every time a broker utters a syllable, he runs the risk of having it jammed down his throat.

In spite of the versatility demanded for success, the broker is usually not rated high in the hierarchy of prestige professions. The public often rates doctors on the highest level, with lawyers, engineers, and scientists somewhat below. Where do we find brokers? Customers have frequently placed them somewhat below racehorse jockeys and slightly above prostitutes. To some the broker is also a grocery clerk filling orders for people entering his store. For some he reaches for the highest shelf while for others he must reach down under the counter.

One of the most common functions of a broker is as a modern whipping boy. In days of yore every noble prince had his favorite companion who was dutifully whipped every time the prince got into trouble. Nowadays every person has his own up-to-date version—his stockbroker. And why not? Anyone should be able to predict the future, know everything about every company, know when a world crisis is going to erupt, predict when a recession is coming, and at the same time make you a million. Anybody who cannot do that deserves his punishment.

Of course, since the earnings of the modern whipping boy range from $15,000 to $350,000 a year, he will gladly bend over regularly. He will accept the blame for your mistakes and praise you for his winners. Although most people have few kind words to say about brokers, they have no choice but to choose one in order to play the market. Here are some of the categories available and hopefully avoidable. If you have thought that brokers are good for nothing, you will discover that they are at least good for a laugh.

Let us stroll into a brokerage house and look around. Notice the broker with the cluttered desk, who also has a cluttered mind. Or the more sophisticated account executive with a clean desk, who isn't doing any business.

Let us stop by the old-timer who has survived the '29 crash. He has suffered through some lean years and tends to be a bit conservative. He cannot understand glamor stocks, and they remain an eternal enigma. He has many war stories that he repeats during every decline, such as how there were so many people jumping out of windows in the '20's that it was dangerous walking along the street. He tries to get with the modern swinging market, and sometimes succeeds. Nevertheless, every evening as he leaves the office building he still looks up.

There are the off-season baseball players and retired athletes. They make excellent brokers. Anyone who can throw a curve can sell stocks. Some of the less talented athletes go on to become insurance and used-car salesmen.

Consider the methodical broker who scientifically sets a daily goal for himself. It may be as much as 1000 shares a day. He is very industrious and devoted to attaining his goals in life. Sometimes, however, the day goes by without an order. Be a little apprehensive if you should get a phone call from him at 3:20 P.M. (2:20 Central time).

Maybe you are fortunate enough to deal with a partner in the firm. You will find him enclosed in a private office, safely insulated from brokerage chatter and far from the madding crowd. He is widely esteemed for never having

"Why did you let me buy AT&T?"

THE STOCKBROKER

been wrong, and is very proud of never having given an opinion. If you should see him at dusk when shadows are falling he can be mistaken for a sphinx.

It is fair to say that brokers as a group are the most honest people in the world. You may laugh at that statement, but there are so many rules and regulations set by the New York Stock Exchange and the Securities Exchange Commission that it is just too much trouble to be dishonest.

The broker is not allowed to churn (trading a customer's account too frequently for the commission). It may be said that a client considers his trading account churned only when it turns into a loser. Since the broker can then be censured verbally and financially, he will strive to avoid the charge. But when things go bad, as they inevitably do, you may find him feverishly scanning his address book, humming "Whom Can I Churn To?"

The broker is an optimistic soul, always seeing a rose-colored world. He has learned years ago that if he becomes bearish in the brokerage business, he may be out of business. Therefore, he is bullish in bull markets, bullish in bear markets, and can be considered one of the few people on this earth who is genuinely full of bull.

Where do brokers come from? Generally, from all walks of life. A business background is useful. A degree adds a little class. Knowledge of the stock market can be helpful. But success in the investment business requires inside information, some family wealth, and rich contacts. Here are some famous men in the world who could be successful brokers:

—Nelson Rockefeller, who could churn himself.

—Howard Hughes, who could buy the Stock Exchange

and turn it into a casino. Few would notice the difference.

—Moishe Dayan, who, with one arm tied behind him and one eye closed, could sell Israeli War Bonds to the Arabs.

—Harold Stassen, who could solicit convention delegates.

Naturally, many aspirants are hired each year. Upon entering the brokerage business, the person is considered a trainee for six months. He studies accounting and finance, learning about balance sheets, current ratios and income statements. He spends months learning the rules of the Exchange which are designed to replace the Ten Commandments. He is thoroughly trained in every facet of the business, from dialing a phone to writing an order. He is systematically taught everything—except how to pick a winner.

After passing the Stock Exchange examinations, the trainee formally enters the business and becomes part of the Organization Chart as seen on the following page. Examine the lowest line, marked with "we's" with a small *w*. These are the forlorn registered representatives who have toiled two to three years, but do not have any rich clients, relatives, or wives. The "we's" are similar to the amoebas, the lowest forms of life, and are comparable to second lieutenants who are expendable in case something goes wrong. On the next line you will find the "We's" with a capital *W*. They are "we's" who have either remarried, latched on to some rich clients, or somehow managed to pick a winner.

Out of all this "we-We" a few become the chosen people —the allied member or junior partner or a "they" with a small *t*. The one indispensable factor in becoming a "they" is money. There are, to be sure, other factors such as the

Organization Chart of a Brokerage House

following, in order of importance: gross commissions, society status, country club affiliation, wife's family, and knowledge.

Once one becomes a partner, life goes on pretty much the same as before, except that there are more meetings, small accounts are disposed of, and one no longer has lunch with former friends known as "we-We's." We then move on to the first really important level, the "They's" with a capital T. They are full partners who are given special administrative positions in the firm. "They's" are often given insulated, walnut-paneled offices so that ticker tapes and news-machine noises do not disturb their daily meditations and occasional naps. Also it can be said that the higher a "They" climbs, the lower his golf score drops.

High above the tumult and the shouting sits the president of the firm. He is ruler supreme of all the "we-We's" and the "they-They's." He is responsible to no one, except, of course, to "god" with a small g, sitting slightly beneath him.

What does this ladder to success prove? It is simply an extension of the "Peter Principle" which stated that everyone rises to his level of incompetence. Applying it to the brokerage hierarchy, we may state its corollary:

*In the brokerage business
mediocrity, like cream, rises straight to the top.*

Now that you have a better understanding of the way brokers think and act, how do they fit into the theoretical system? It has been noted that brokers perform a multitude of services, at various times functioning as psychiatrist, marriage counselor, divorce judge, and market seer. But the basic brokerage function is simply that of a redistributor or middleman, bringing together buyer and seller and insider and outsider. He is an essential link in the redistribution process helping the flow of money out of one wallet and into another. He does not reason why, he simply sells and buys. He aids both *distributor* and *distributee,* serving either for a fee.

The broker is devoted to his work and to your money. He is always at your call, and you may ask anything of him—his time, his loyalty, his sanity . . . but, always remember this brokerage principle:

*Ask not what your broker can do for you,
ask what you can do for your broker.*

2
The Co-Redistributors

"To err is human, to forgive divine."
Alexander Pope

The Advisory Services and Security Analysts

IN ANCIENT days, the world depended on soothsayers, astrologers, and oracles to divine the future. When the age of the stock market dawned, new prophets were needed to give guidance in a modern world. Crystal balls were replaced by computers, and ouija boards gave way to charts as the advisory services and security analysts became the fortunetellers of finance in the Age of Aquarius.

It is always easier to be a fortuneteller than a "fortunedoer." The market visionary can usually see more clearly for others than for himself. He feels that he has a mission in life to help others attain their goals. He believes that he performs the essential function of helping investors to see in advance why they may get redistributed.

These purveyors of advice have much in common. They prefer to be considered researchers rather than soothsayers, disclaiming any supernatural talents and basing everything on the scientific sifting of facts. In this manner they have raised the art of fortunetelling to the sophisticated science of research, producing a prodigious output of reports, write-ups, and analyses. Though operating independently, they have the uncanny faculty of thinking, talking, and acting alike. They are unanimous in recommending the same stocks on the way up and dumping them on the way down. Although this action may result in a sheep syndrome, it does yield unexpected blessings, for when you've taken advice from one, you've had it from all.

Let us look at the various kinds of crystal balls and see how they help the market flow along.

THE ADVISORY SERVICES

The services are the most regular advice-givers, making weekly and monthly recommendations for a modest fee. For a hundred dollars they will gladly give you advice on making a million. Hopefully, with 10,000 subscribers they, too, can garner a million. Here are some kinds of investment ideas you may receive:

There is the "buckshot" approach. The idea is to mention as many stocks as possible, spraying names all over the place. Then in subsequent letters the hits, or winners, are mentioned again, while the misses, or losers, are dismissed into limbo.

In the "hedge" method the service gives guarded advice, cautioning investors with a host of caveats. On the first page the market in general may be described as forming a top with 87% of the service's indicators pointing down predicting a severe decline to the 480 level over the next few years. On the following page, five stocks are recommended for long-term appreciation. One stock may be suitable for aggressive investors, but completely inappropriate for chicken investors. It may be confidently purchased by long-term accounts, if they don't mind losing in the short term. Each person is thus warned of the consequences of acting on the recommendation and, if he still follows it, deserves to be distributed.

The most famous service is that of the Market Cassandra who direly predicts gloom, doom and a crash. He usually begins issuing his warning at the beginning of the decade, say the spring of 1921, and finally becomes famous and widely quoted in the fall of '29. Though he may have missed a couple of roaring bull markets, he is widely esteemed for having finally been right. Some of the more patient Cassandras have had to wait twenty or thirty years for their crash to come in, 1970 being a most rewarding year. This type is known as the "If You're Bearish Long Enough, You've Got to Be Right" service.

There is also the "Follow the Leader" recommendation, which selects the most popular stock under the assumption and hope that the other services will follow. This may be considered a sophisticated application of *The Bigger Fool Theory*.

The services strive to do their best, hoping you will be pleased enough to resubscribe. They will point out how much you need to be kept informed. Their most compelling argument, however, is that their yearly fee, like their results, is tax deductible.

THE SECURITY ANALYSTS

Another kind of market prophet is the analyst. He is the pride of the brokerage house, and is sometimes known as the research analyst, investment analyst, statistician and all-round tipster. He is usually a frustrated writer, who, never having succeeded commercially in writing fiction, turns to writing stock analyses.

The analyst is hired by brokerage houses, banks and mutual funds. He is responsible for doing research on companies, visiting them, meeting management and making projections of future earnings. He is supposed to write up his conclusions of whether to buy, hold or sell the stock.

One of his most important functions is to comment on the daily market activity. The final edition of every major newspaper carries a financial commentary on the day's events as a public service. It is hoped that investors who understand the market action will make sounder decisions. Once they are familiar with the popular phrases, they soon discover a ten-day market cycle:

Assuming there has been a substantial decline in the previous week the first day of any rally is described as "technical" meaning there is no evident reason for the rise other than "what goes down, goes up" eventually.

The second day of the rally is called a "continuation of the technical rebound," helped by a large amount of short covering.

By the third day the analysts begin to speak of "renewed investor confidence" in that there is hope that interest rates have peaked, the economy is stronger than anticipated, and more troop withdrawals are coming.

The fourth day is termed an "extension of the uptrend" with another rise of 30 to 40 points in the averages expected as "investor confidence" continues to rise.

The fifth day brings many "buy" recommendations of "selected, well-situated" securities that are behind the market in that they have not, as yet, participated in the rise.

These optimistic pronouncements coincide with the decline on the sixth day called "profit-taking" which is considered normal after such a rise.

The seventh day brings another drop which is viewed as "constructive," for it is a base being formed to launch future gains.

The plunge of the eighth day is termed a "consolidation" of the previous week's rally, which is necessary before any sustained rise in prices can be achieved.

The price erosion of the ninth day is explained as a need to "test the previous lows" before "investor confidence" can have any confidence. The panic of the tenth day is simply a return to "gloomy investor psychology" based on fears of higher interest rates, a softening economy and expansion of the war.

The analytical cycle has its uses, for any sharp investor realizes that the analysts help forecast the future in spite of themselves. You can reliably predict that panics will lead to technical rebounds followed by optimistic recommendations which inevitably lead to profit-taking, consolidations and bottom-testing. Although everything you know is what you read in the newspapers, the key to success is knowing how to read them.

Consider the poor analyst who has the job of issuing both a morning comment for his brokerage house, and an analysis after the close for the daily newspaper.

He wakes up in the morning after his usual miserable night's sleep, glances around at his over-mortgaged house and his overweight wife and yawns, "Gee, I feel bearish." Why shouldn't he feel low? He's been in a bear market for two years, is worried about his job, and has lost half his capital. He has also gone short (borrowing a stock, selling it out and hoping to rebuy it at a lower price), and hopes to benefit from a further decline. Unfortunately, the market has been rallying for two weeks since it hit its low of 631 and he is beginning to worry about the other half of his capital.

He gets to his office early and picks up the *Wall Street Journal* for background information. Suddenly tears of happiness well up in his bearish eyes when he reads that General Motors has gone on strike. Inspired, he quickly writes his commentary: "Look for early weakness on increased volume with an intra-day rally occurring after the first hour. The downtrend should resume by mid-session and expect generally deteriorating prices toward the close as the dire economic consequences of the auto strike begin to filter through the investment community."

He sends out his report to the salesmen in all the firm's offices, and finally relaxes, hibernating in his private office. He is a bit surprised when he notices the market up 4.82 on the opening with large buyers predominating. He is astonished at the noon averages being up 8.72 and slumps into his chair at the up 12.47 closing.

He slowly types out his market résumé and just beats the deadline for the final edition of the newspaper:

"The market showed unexpected strength today closing up 12.47. Volume surged on 17,800,000 shares. The underlying strength in the market was underscored by the positive reaction to the General Motors strike. Investors are regarding it as beneficial to the economy as it helps to cool inflation and reduce interest rates. It was also noted that extensive short covering by scared bears helped fuel the rally."

The analyst also is well known as a frustrated fiction writer. He approaches his analysis as a novelist does his novel. His characters are company presidents, treasurers, and accountants. His stories are necessarily long, most investors equating a story's weight with its worth. His work is so creatively written that one may read on, never knowing fact from fiction.

He can coin a phrase with the best of writers:

"Risk-Reward Ratio," or the odds of ever getting your money back.

A "Concept Stock," or one with a story about it so technically difficult to understand that the analyst has not the foggiest concept of what it is all about.

"Synergism," an erotic attraction between two companies which brings them together to give birth to an erratic third.

"The Sophisticated Investor," or one who possesses the calm wisdom to invest for the long term, remaining cool to rumors of a quarterly company loss, medium cool to a temporary market plunge and ice cold at the news that his most "sophisticated stock," Penn Central, has declared bankruptcy.

A "Value," the price of a stock so low in relation to its intrinsic worth that you cannot understand why it is selling so cheaply; but at the same time you fear buying it because it may become undervalued.

"Earnings Estimate," a vision of next year's earnings, a dream, something devoutly to be wished.

"Earnings Visibility," the ability to be foresighted about earnings when the stock is rising, nearsighted when the stock is dropping, and blind when it falls out of bed.

"Hedge Fund," a formula for investment wherein the stocks bought long go down, and the ones sold short go up, thus seeking a third method of losing.

In creating his "story," the analyst's most important tool for plotting is the "earnings visibility" or earnings projection. Once he has an earnings estimate for next year, and the next, and a few others, he becomes convinced of the potential for the stock and issues a "buy" recommendation. This means "earnings visibility" is unlimited, say $2.00 this year and $4.00 next, with the stock doubling each year. On a clear up market he can see forever.

The plot and the visibility thicken as the year progresses. When the stock begins to drop, the first conflict arises between the characters in the story. The analyst calls the company president to check if there is anything wrong.

"I know of no reason for the decline in our stock."

"Are you sure there are no new developments?" the analyst pleads.

"I know of no reason . . ."

Irritated, the analyst changes his recommendation to "hold" which means he would prefer making it "sell," but dislikes ruining his contact with the company by offending top management.

He salves his conscience by lowering his projections to $1.50 this year, $3.00 next, maybe. The drama is heightened by the analyst becoming disenchanted with the president and the president becoming cool to the analyst. As the stock drops further the president still doesn't know why. Ten points lower and he cannot be reached by phone.

The climax comes in a surprise ending worthy of O. Henry. The company loses $2.00 and hopes to double it next year. The tragic but heroic security analyst can write the book on any stock, except chapter 11. In the throes of despair he issues a "sell" recommendation as the stock plunges downward, faster, ever so swiftly until—

Ceiling Zero

THE CHARTISTS

Like fortune tellers gazing into their crystal balls and astrologers scanning the heavens, the chartists of the market place peer intently into their graph paper, envisioning omens of good or bad markets. Shunning conventional statistical data, they draw "point and figure" charts by meticulously plotting the highs and lows of the stock over a period of time. By analyzing the mistakes of the past, they are able to extrapolate them into the future.

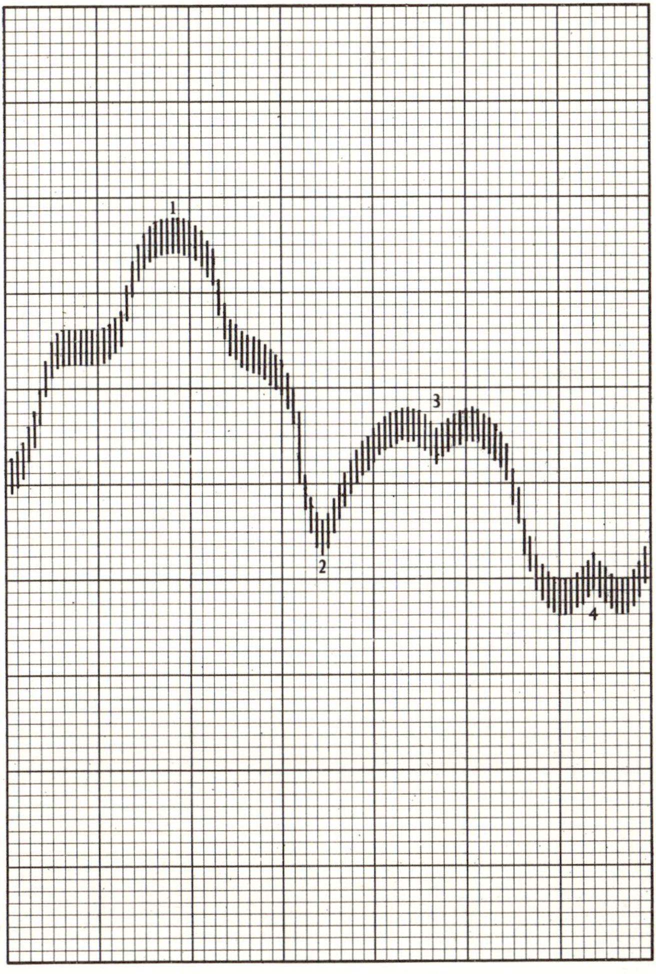
1
2
3
4

But what is it they actually see? Mysterious signs? Portents of the future? Or perhaps some reflection of their subconscious. Let us take a look at a typical chart, on the preceding page, and through a little detective work see if we can discover what it really portrays.

Let us divide *Bobbie Brooks* into distinct patterns as the chartists like to do. Employing their terminology, we shall reassemble the shapes into a more revealing form. Let us begin with form 1)

The Head and Shoulders

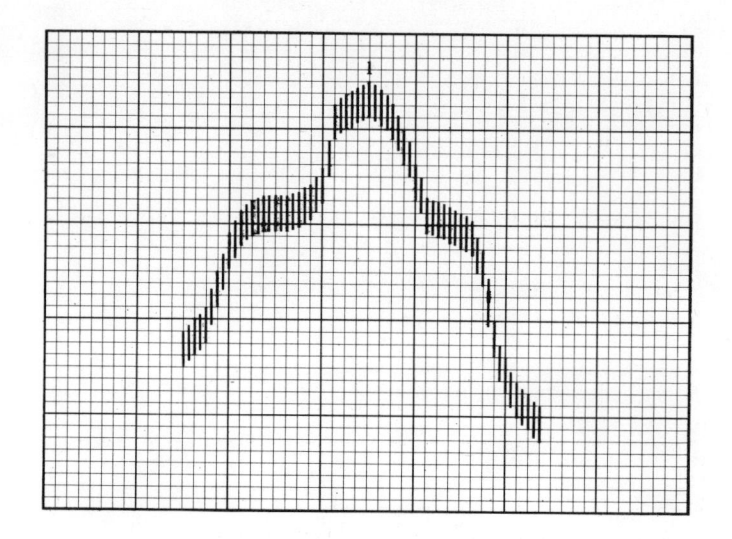

We may easily recognize the outline of the chartist's favorite Head and Shoulders figure. We may also discern that he is no longer simply tracing a hot stock; rather, he is indulging himself in his favorite pastime—drawing girlie pictures. He is aroused when he follows the neckline, for when it curves down over the shoulder, he knows she's going down.

Proceeding down on the chart at 2) we come to the familiar

V Formation

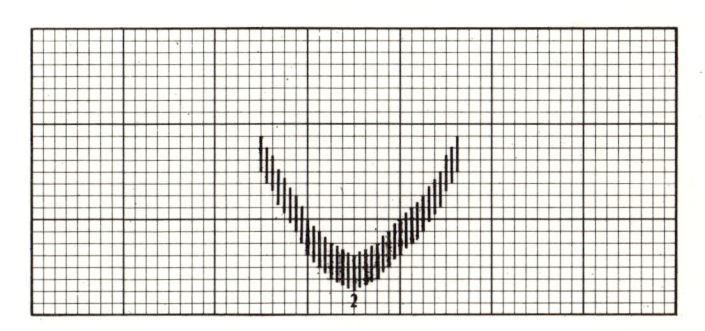

which simply shows that what plunges down can quickly snap up.

As we head down, we come across another stimulating formation:

The Double Top

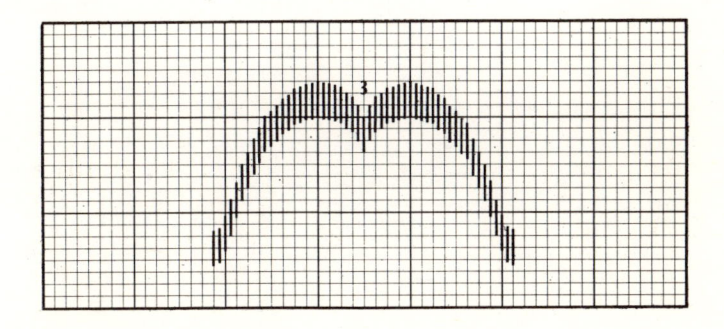

Many chartists have gone wild over the form and have been frequently sucked in near the high. Others look for another shape to hop on:

The Double Bottom

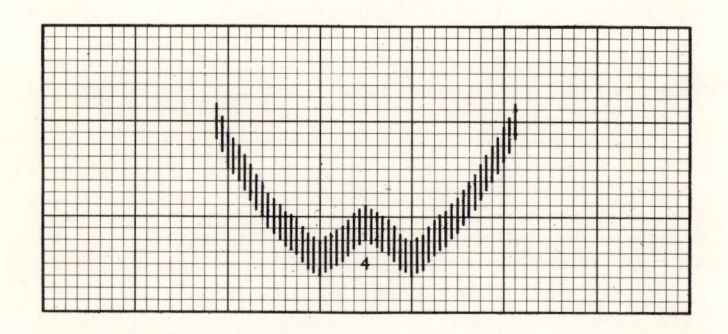

The more adroit chartists will tell you that a good "Saucer Bottom" will provide firm support for any upward movement. Tops and Bottoms have always been popular, but the more erotic chartists only go wild over "Triple Tops" and "Triple Bottoms."

Now let us combine these forms into a more recognizable shape to illustrate the chartist's favorite glamor stock or dream girl (see facing page).

You may have difficulty finding this chart pattern in your brokerage house. It is rarely found in the technical market letters or advisory services. It is sometimes seen over-the-counter and sold under-the-counter. If you can't find your favorite pattern in any financial magazine, do not be alarmed. Simply unfold the centerpiece of your *Playboy* magazine.

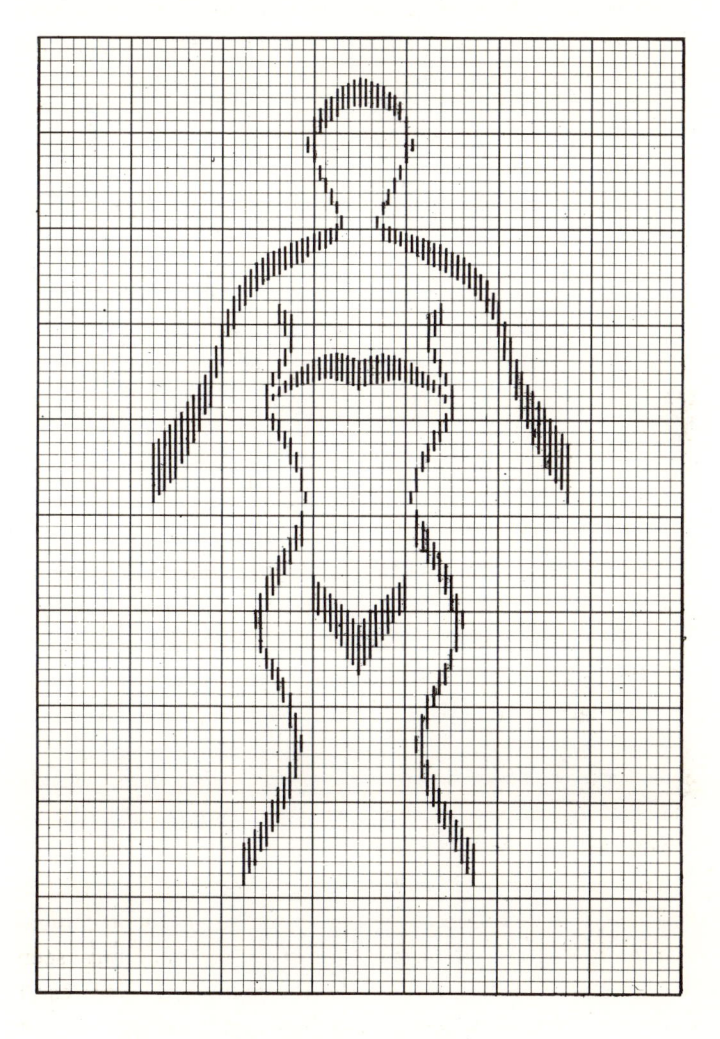

Miss Bobbie Brooks (Pin-Up Version)
Apologies to *Playboy*

The Advisory Services and Security Analysts are thus seen to be catalysts for the market, stirring up enthusiasm for the cycle. The market needs a steady infusion of new money to keep moving forward and this group helps to channel it in the proper direction. At the same time they remain aloof. Like the brokers, they prefer to remain outside the market so that they are not affected by its ups and downs. In this manner they have become a steadying force, always able to give advice during each period, whether bull or bear. They will always remain steadfast and untouchable, as long as they wisely refrain from taking their own advice.

HURRY UP, WE NEED OUR SHORT TERM BUY LIST
JUST A MINUTE.. I THINK WE'RE GONNA HIT TODAY
Wall Street Journal
POLAROID
MEMOREX
CONTROL DATA
TELEX

3
A Friend in Need

> "Many are called, few are chosen."
> Cassius Clay

Borrowing From a Banker
or
How to Stop Living, and Start Worrying

BANKERS MAY be classified as the most amiable and congenial of the *redistributors*. They are eager to be of service, allowing you to borrow at your will and pay it back at theirs. Their doors are open to all, welcoming both *distributor* and *distributee*, financing them, advising them, and sometimes helping them change places.

They are true men of principal—always watching yours and preserving theirs. In the course of time they have helped redistribute more capital than any other group. At the same time they have remained undistributable, for they follow a simple banking commandment:

> *Thou shalt never own a stock,*
> *when thou mayest call a loan.*

This has allowed most bankers to survive most market declines. Of course, when they do not obey this edict, they, too, can be decapitalized. Therefore, although they hold vast amounts of collateralized stock, they abhor the idea of ever owning one share.

If you should decide to borrow, you may walk into the

office of your friendly banker, and ask him for your first loan. He will greet you with the congeniality of a gracious host, and will be delighted to make you a generous loan. This will enable you to buy on margin or to borrow more than you are worth. This is what is known as leverage. Buying on margin magnifies the potential for gain by giving you a chance to make a fortune with a small amount of capital. If you should lose, however, you could pay thousands of dollars in yearly interest for the honor of losing your fanny.

Your banker will immediately put you at ease and explain how all the facilities of the bank are at your disposal. He will have you sign a note which will be secured by your stocks, bonds, or blood. Upon signing he will cart out a gift for you, to show you his gratitude:

Congratulations!
Here Is Your Gift for Dealing with Us
May You Have Many Hours of Enjoyment

One
Portable
Do It Yourself . . .
Guillotine Kit

Please follow directions carefully:

You should first mount the platform on a flat surface, preferably with good drainage. This step should coincide with your first $10,000 loan in a rising market.

Next, place the block on the platform and take out a $20,000 loan. Things are really looking up.

Then with the help of your friendly broker, erect the scaffolding and insert blade; increase loan to $40,000 and take a comfortable nap on the block, while awaiting a new era for stock prices.

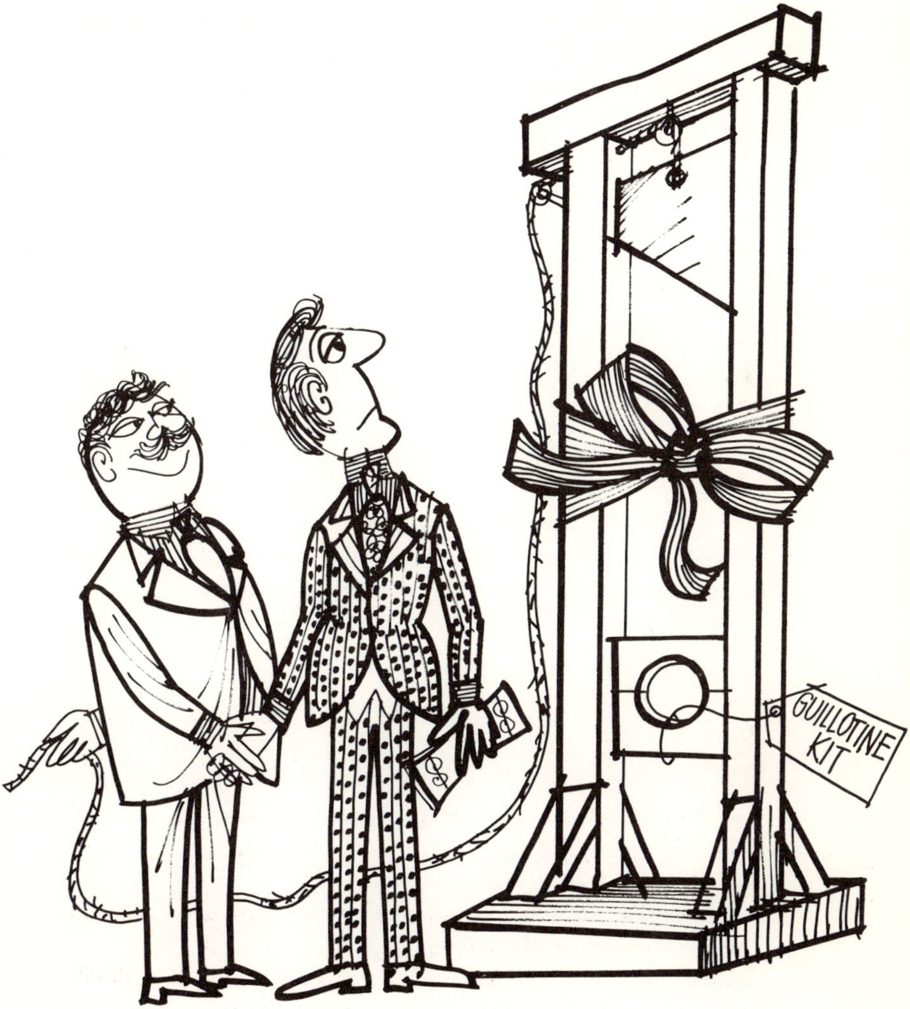
GUILLOTINE KIT

Finally, when all the brokers are bullish, the advisory services are unanimously optimistic, and the economy is booming, take out an $80,000 loan to make a real killing in the market.

Suddenly the fair weather passes, the storm roars in, the market crashes, and both your equity and the guillotine begin to fall. You would never pull the lever, but the executioner has arrived. You have made your guillotine, and your friendly banker, like a warden in a prison, must do his duty.

Every time there is a severe market decline, there are a large number of executions. The number of do-it-yourself kits increased sharply in 1929, 1938, 1962, 1966, and 1970. It is amazing how the market always comes back, but how few people are able to glue their heads back on.

Practically speaking, the only way to feel secure is to borrow so much that you control too much of a stock. If the banker decides to sell such a block, he could conceivably distribute himself in a declining market. He will probably conclude that it is better to lend you more, rather than pulling the guillotine lever. This leads to our first borrowing principle:

Either borrow so much that
if you sneeze the banker trembles
or
so little that you may
thumb your running nose at him

Although most people borrow on stocks, only the most sophisticated buy convertible bonds on margin. The bond buyer disdains the stock buyer by chanting a little ditty:

"There are stocks
And there are blondes,
But gentlemen prefer bonds."

A convertible bond is a debt of a company, a kind of promissory note. It has a magical quality about it. It is supposed to be a bond when the market is down, but turns into a stock when the market is up.

Many convertible buyers feel they cannot lose because of the company's promise to repay the bond at a certain maturity date. Consider the many maturing in 1984. How George Orwell would have shuddered waiting to get his money back!

A best-selling book by a Canadian doctor has recently aroused great interest in convertible bonds. The doctor stated that with $400 anyone can make a million. Perhaps by borrowing and through brilliant maneuvering he did make a million. But who ever heard of a doctor with $400?

Bankers, like brokers, may be classified as *redistributors of wealth*. They are eager to help the economy flow along. They perform a valuable service and are always ready to help you at almost any time, except the time you really need them.

Bankers are always sympathetic to a person of high integrity. But unfortunately, your honor is safe; it is your loan that is in danger. On the market pendulum many are called (unfortunately by their margin clerk or banker), but few are chosen to reach the golden rainbow. Whether it be a stock, a bond, or a blonde, don't lose your head over any of them. Remember these borrowing principles:

Better to be liquid than liquidated
and
Beware of bankers bearing gifts.

Two

THE DISTRIBUTEE

or
He Who Gets Distributed All Over
the Ticker Tape

> "Fools rush in where Angels fear to tread."
> General George Custer

The Rationale of Irrational Man

THE DISTRIBUTEE is the epitome of "Irrational Man." He thinks not with his head, but with his heart. He is driven into the market by the force of human emotions. He is a man of many moods, euphorically buying at market highs and despondently selling at market lows. He is sometimes manic, sometimes depressive, a bit schizophrenic, and gradually over the years becomes an impotent investor.

He is also a masochist in disguise, whipping himself with losing trades, bleeding himself continually of his capital, and all the while enjoying every downtick. He is courted avidly by the insiders who enjoy distributing their stocks to him at the highs and buying them back near the lows. He is loved by traders who whipsaw him in up-and-down markets, and adored by brokers who admire anyone who can efficiently churn himself.

His abnormal actions are not too difficult to understand. He is obsessed with rising above his class, and would like to move out fast. When he tries to trade quickly, the commissions seem to eat up his capital. Even when he hits, taxes eat up his gains. In his quest for the easy money, he is frustrated at every turn.

So he turns into a long-term investor, trying to ignore the temporary fluctuations. He has read somewhere that fortunes have been made only through patient holding for capital gains. This will allow him to pay a lower tax rate if he can survive for six months. The trouble is that the longer he holds, the more neurotic he tends to become. His nerves are on edge as he daily faces the threats of assassination, presidential heart attacks, war scares, and hijackings. He personally feels each crisis through the price fluctuations of his stocks. He becomes high strung like a man on a hot thin tightrope:

Unnerved by rumors and by declining markets he trembles on. It is no surprise then that even the way he talks reveals certain abnormalities. Here are some actual phone conversations with his favorite broker and their psychiatric thin tightrope.

Upon hearing a broker's recommendation to buy:
"Let's watch it awhile," or "Let's see how it acts." (I really don't want it, but I hate to hurt my broker's feelings. If it goes up, it will be too high to buy. If it goes down, I'll be so deliriously happy that I didn't listen to him.)

"Send me a Standard and Poor's ticket." (I'll humor him along. I still don't want it, but maybe I can find some reason in print for not liking it.)

"O.K., let's put a bid under the market." (I hope I don't get it and I pray he calls me when it gets within a quarter of a point of my order so I can lower it and make sure I never own it.)

Upon owning a certain stock:
"I'm not selling, I'm a long termer." (As long as it's up I'm holding, but if it gets near my cost I'm running, or, I

LOSS OF PROFIT WORRIES
WAR SCARE
MARKET RUMORS
ASSASSINATIONS
SIX MONTH-LONG TERM CAPITAL GAIN TIGHTROPE
LACK OF NERVE
$

can't afford the loss; I'm holding 'til I get my money back.)

"Let's put a sell order above the market." (I hope I can raise the order before it's sold, because I don't really want to sell it unless I get the absolute high.)

When he has a profit:
"I'm holding for a capital gain, just a month to go."
"I know it's a capital gain, but since it's December, let's wait and put it in next year's taxes."
"I can't sell it now, look how far it's gone down since December."

After selling the stock:
"I can always buy it back cheaper." (I hope the guy who bought it loses his fanny, and if it does go down, I'll really be too scared to buy it back.)

The *distributee* is better known as the little guy, the sometimes round- but mostly odd-lotter, the lovable but gullible small investor, who is encouraged to buy a share in the future of America just when it is turning bleak.

He is the most loyal member of the system, completely dedicated to the idea that easy money lies somewhere over the ticker-tape. Consequently, everyone is eager to help him reach his goals and displays great interest in his welfare.

Security analysts carefully watch his odd-lot behavior, studying his buying patterns so that they may develop their selling patterns.

The brokers try to help him along by charging an extra eighth or quarter on odd lots, and by raising his commissions.

He chases after hot new issues always looking for that really hot meal, but the underwriters give him all the cold cuts he can eat.

THE RATIONALE OF IRRATIONAL MAN

The option writer welcomes his interest in puts and calls and allows him to acquire a large amount of stock for a small amount of money. The option writer is happy to write the call and put it to him.

With all these concerned market friends there is no need for financial enemies. To be sure there are people who admire the fortitude of the little guy and have devoted their life to studying his behavior. It has been discovered that there are as many variations as there are butterflies. A noted collector has catalogued them under their scientific name, *Amateuris Investoris*. Here is a listing of the most common types.

1) The Bad Loser. Considers a $100 loss a calamity; when he makes $200, "Eh, it's nothing."

2) The Cyclical Amateur. He has his own private cycle:
"It's a fool's rally." (Count me in.)
"They're dropping now." (Count me out.)
"They're up again." (Count me in again.)

3) The Manic-Depressive. Well known for checking quotes five times a day. Gradually becomes a bit manic-depressive while his stock gyrates during the market session. His favorite phrases are "Ah! Oh! Oi!"

4) The Wall Street Waltzer. He dances from stock to stock to the music of the "Wall Street Waltz":
—A one,
and a two,
and a three,
and—*Trip*.

5) Hope Springs Eternal. When he sells a stock, he hopes it will go to hell. It gives him great delight to know

that thousands of people who bought when he sold have lost their assets.

6) Going Broke Taking a Profit. There is the poor fellow who feels himself losing while winning. If he owns five hundred shares of stock at a cost of 10 and it rises to 30, he has a $10,000 profit at the high. The stock suddenly drops back to 20.

"I lost $5,000," he cries.

"How can you lose when you're ahead," the broker wonders.

"But I'm losing money every day."

"Then take your profit at 20."

"It might go back to 30."

"Then you'll be out $10,000," mumbles the broker all the way to the psychiatrist.

7) The Panic Pusher. When calamity strikes, and the stock plummets precipitously several days in a row, he panics and throws in his sell order at the low. Then, as the stock roars back up in the eventual rally, he feels like a man who has missed his plane.

8) The Market Curse. There is nothing worse than selling a stock that continues to climb every day. It simply drives this type crazy. Each day he picks up the stock page with trembling fingers and winces when he sees his former favorite up another 2 points. He becomes a man possessed. "I have to buy it back," he cries out. "What if it goes higher?" he thunders. For months, years, he feels a twinge in his heart at the sound of that damned stock. If he is really conscientious, it becomes a curse on him.

9) The Market Butterfly. There is the butterfly who

gaily flies from blossom to blossom, from stock to stock, and broker to broker. He is continually swayed by the aroma of high volume, rumors, and fairy tales. Nothing is more delightful than catching a butterfly in a brokerage house, for the broker usually winds up spinning himself a cocoon of churned commissions.

10) The Breakfast Blitzkrieg. The husband and wife who trade together, do not necessarily stay together. He is calm, cool, and can pick his winners if left alone. However, it is the breakfast blitzkrieg which unnerves him. Every morning his wife screams over the coffee, "It's going down. What are you going to do about it?"

"It's a blue chip," he replies. "It'll go back up."

"We'll lose everything. I'll have to go back to work."

"It's yielding 5%."

"I could have bought a second car with the money. But no, you had to squander it in the stock market. How can you be so cruel to me?"

"Sell the god-damned thing."

11) Group Mediocrity. The Investment Club represents a special type of investing. Group mediocrity is substituted for individual mediocrity. It is the purest form of democratic government, allowing the most senseless investment ideas to be voted on by the majority of the most senseless members.

12) The Track Star. In every boardroom, one finds the track star, who is always running to keep ahead of the last sale on the tape. Wherever he places his sale order, he lifts the price immediately whenever the stock rises within two points of the order. He scampers continually to keep his

The Butterfly
Species: *Amateuris Investoris*

order in the lead. He hates to be caught. He runs a good race and usually does not really want to sell until he finds nobody is chasing him any longer. He then turns around and chases the falling prices, keeping his offer two points above the last sale. The falling stock then becomes the new track star.

13) The Cherished Dreamer. One finds the investor who thinks of his profits in terms of his cherished dream. When he buys a thousand shares of a stock at 10 and it goes to 30, he does not think of his $20,000 profit, but rather of his dream home with three bedrooms and two bathrooms. When the stock goes to 33 he mentally adds two rooms. At 37 there are four johns and a large garage. Suddenly the stock drops to 31. Two of the rooms are suddenly gone. Another day and it is 24 and two bathrooms disappear. At 20 there are no johns. At last there is a rally. The stock and the houses are both going back up. The stock rebounds to 30. "I just got two johns back." At 40 "I'm adding an extra room."

14) Chicken Little. Finally there is Chicken Little who runs scared everytime he buys a stock. Whenever there is a downtick he quacks, "Dear me the sky is falling, I think I'll call my broker."

Although we have taken a lighthearted look at the *distributee*, it is important to realize that he plays a serious role in our economy. Without him no one could get rich. There would be no one to distribute stocks to at the highs. Volume would dry up. Brokers would go broke. The whole economic system would collapse. Call him what you wish— the little guy, "Irrational Man", or *distributee*—he is still the key element in the system.

You may find him anywhere—along Wall Street, Main Street or even your street. The only place you may never find him is in your hall mirror.

The Irrational Check List

This page is filled with blanks so that you can play "Match Your Favorite Irrational Man" with your favorite irrational friend.

1) The Bad Loser   _____
2) The Cyclical Amateur   _____
3) The Manic-Depressive   _____
4) The Wall Street Waltzer _____
5) Hope Springs Eternal   _____
6) Going Broke Taking a Profit _____
7) The Panic Pusher   _____
8) The Market Curse   _____
9) The Market Butterfly   _____
10) The Breakfast Blitzkrieg _____
11) Group Mediocrity   _____
12) The Track Star   _____
13) The Cherished Dreamer _____
14) Chicken Little   _____

If you can match 14, rate yourself excellent, 10—good, 7—average, 3—mediocre, and 0—you have no friends; call a broker immediately.

Three

THE DISTRIBUTORS

Completing the Cycle

HAVING ANALYZED and psychoanalyzed the *distributee*, it is time that we, like a good broker, bring the *distributee* and the *distributor* together. Once joined they will act and react together creating a cyclical movement as the money flows like the tides into one pocket and out another.

There are many kinds of *distributors* operating in this cycle and each is an expert in applying the redistribution theory. They know that to sell thousands of shares of stock at high prices requires the stirring up of great enthusiasm among the mass of investors. They know the driving force that emotions play. Only mad fits of passion could account for so many people losing their money and their reason.

They have similar traits. They all buy stocks at a fraction of the price the public pays. They prefer not to buy anyone else's stock, hoping that everyone will buy theirs. They have access to inside information and know what they are doing at all times. Consequently, their most common trait is that they rarely lose.

Let us study four main categories of *distributors* and see how they use different types of human emotions in their operations. The first distributor has become a legend in history, his financial exploits having made him justly famous on Wall Street.

1
The Secondary Distributor

"What the public knows about the stock market is worthy of being written on the honored walls of a john."

Howard Hughes

The Invisible Hand

OUR FIRST distributor has the ability to distribute stocks smoothly and effortlessly. He also possesses a *savoir-faire* rare to the market. The most successful example of this genre is Howard Hughes who many believe to be a reincarnation of Adam Smith's "Invisible Hand," quietly and efficiently guiding the economy of the nation. While operating imperceptively behind the scenes, he accomplished the incredible feat of single-handedly redistributing Wall Street.

For years Howard Hughes had been the mystery man of the financial world and the controlling power of Transworld Airlines. He had not been seen in public for so many years that many doubted he ever existed. The TWA directors even wondered, for they had not seen him in decades. So it was a surprise in 1966 when Howard Hughes, the biggest stockholder of TWA, announced that he would sell out all his holdings, personally.

Traditionally, the pundits of Wall Street have agreed that what was good for Howard was bad for TWA. If the airline had a mediocre record, it was his fault. If the stock did not perform well, again it was his doings. It became the fashion of the day for airline analysts to blame Howard for all Transworld's ills.

Suits were filed in court to wrest control of TWA away from Howard. But he naturally never showed up. He was thus faced with the enmity of investors, the malice of analysts, and the contempt of court. But Howard Hughes was practical. He sneaked into the dark recesses of the executives' washroom at TWA, where he made many decisions. He meditated in his private office and jumped to the conclusion that the investment community would win. They would force him to sell out at the high.

The news of the impending sale electrified Wall Street. Everyone was eager for Hughes' stock, even if he were a bit shy about selling. If Howard Hughes would not come to the public, then the public would come to Howard Hughes.

A question lingered over the market. How could a man quietly sell 6,500,000 shares of stock? Would he deliver the stock, much less sign it? No one guaranteed anything, except that he would collect the money.

Howard Hughes' advisors were shocked. After all, he owned 86% of the stock and they reasoned that such a block of stock would depress the market. But Howard knew better. He understood "irrational man." He knew instinctively that he could count on another propelling emotional force:

"They hate me so much, they'll bid up the price to get rid of me."

To be sure he needed help, and he received it through a selling technique popular with brokerage houses. It is officially known as a "secondary distribution" or selling a block of stock through individual brokers to their customers at a net price. It is the most sincere and honest form of distribution, for it is the only time that you are told in advance exactly how and at what price you are going to be distributed.

And so it was to be. Hughes' stock would be sold via a secondary offering through the brokers of America (functioning as the redistributors of wealth). The brokers were happy with their big commission, analysts were delighted with their analyses, and investors were ready to rush in. Few worried why Howard wanted to trade.

In the conference rooms across the nation some big mutual funds considered buying. But they were sophisticated buyers and needed facts, analyses, and earnings projections before making big buying decisions.

The senior analyst of one fund decided the job was too big for any man. So he bought a computer. It was the biggest and best available. He regarded the computer as created in his own image and proceeded to program his head into it.

The analyst computer had great advantages. It could work 24 hours a day without sex. It could chart a stock without a ruler. It could select the likely market winners in a flash, since it had all the financial knowledge of the world at its circuit tips. And it certainly could not make an error, inasmuch as the computer was purchased from a firm secretly owned by Howard Hughes.

The senior analyst and his assistants huddled around the computer, affectionately named Mack Jr.:

"What looks good, Mack?"

"TWA."

"Why do you like it?"

"Sixteen times earnings, 8 times cash flow, 4 times book

"Fools rushed in where Howard feared to fly."

value, and should double according to the chart."
"Is the timing right?"
"Certainly, Howard Hughes is selling out. Without him TWA can take off."
"Good, order 200,000 shares of the secondary at 86. . . ."
Three years later and about to hit the silk at 21.
"What went wrong, Mack?"
Silence.
"I said what went wrong?"
Silence.
"You can't make a mistake. If you don't talk, I'm going to smash your dials."
"To err is human, to forgive divine."
"Forgive? We lost a fortune. You said the company would soar without Hughes. How could you be so wrong? Look at the millions we spent having you built."
"You get what you pay for."
"But I programmed you with my head. How could you come up with such garbage?"
"What you put in, you get out."
"I could talk to myself and get better answers. I'm going to electronically castrate you."
"You wouldn't dare*eeeeeowh*."
"I'm going to smash you with my rulers," roared the assistant analyst.
"I'm going to short your circuits," shouted another.
Mack the Computer, dying, looked down from his drooping dials. . . .
The "secondary distribution" was indeed a great financial success—for the underwriters, the brokers, and Howard's bank balance. Hughes also gained wide recognition as the finest airline analyst of our times. With such renown you

may wonder why Howard chose to remain an invisible man. He is not the mystery man you may think nor is he really antisocial. It is simply that if you had personally distributed over $400 million worth of stock near the high, you'd be hiding too.

2
The Distributors of Glamor Stocks and the Cycle of Love

> "'Tis better to have loved and lost
> than never to have loved at all."
>
> Tommy Manville

The Making of a Glamor Stock

IN THE olden, golden days of the twenties, stocks were manipulated freely and with malice toward all. Then came the crash, the investigations and all the laws that try to keep one from making money in the market. All the buying pools and bear raiders went into hiding. There arose their legitimate heirs—the entrepreneurial promotors who have mastered the fine art of pushing up a stock without really buying it.

The promotor knows the distribution cycle well and in this case depends on another emotional force: love. He becomes a Hollywood-type mogul and sets out to turn an obscure dog into a well-known glamor stock. He knows that with the right publicity and build-up the public will fall in love with his protégée.

He must first find the right vehicle for her, which is usually a relatively unknown company, sitting dormant in the over-the-counter market. With a small amount of his own capital and a lot of his friends', he buys control and begins a scenario worthy of Hollywood.

He quickly changes the name. What's in a name? Oh,

about 10 points on Wall Street. Garbage collectors become Pollution Controllers. Sewage disposal changes into Industrial Services. Bedsprings Incorporated transforms into Reproductions, Inc.

He composes a theme song for his production number:

"Praise the Lord and pass the ammunition,
Let's go out and make an acquisition."

He hums it as he woos bit players to join his company. He borrows money from bankers to swing deals as fast as possible. If the area he is in goes out of favor, he tries to buy companies that are in favor. When computer leases expire, he goes after Indonesian Oil. When oil wells go dry, he builds mobile homes. These opportune acquisitions always manage to add to sales, and occasionally to earnings.

The mogul hires an accounting firm to help with her figure. He knows that the accountants are part-time beauticians and magicians. They can beautify any set of numbers as if by magic. They can take an expense and capitalize it into an asset. Or they can just as easily take the asset and accelerate the depreciation, turning a loss into a profit. If there are too many red wrinkles, he can change LIFO into FIFO and in desperation, KNIFO. Her most beautiful figure is thus most easily put forward.

He also hires a public relations firm to spread the word. Earnings guesstimates are bandied about, new products are hinted at, and features articles on management appear in magazines and newspapers. The entrepreneurial promoter-president begins to make the rounds of security analysts meetings. Free publicity and a free lunch never hurt anyone. He notices that every time he gives a speech the stock rises

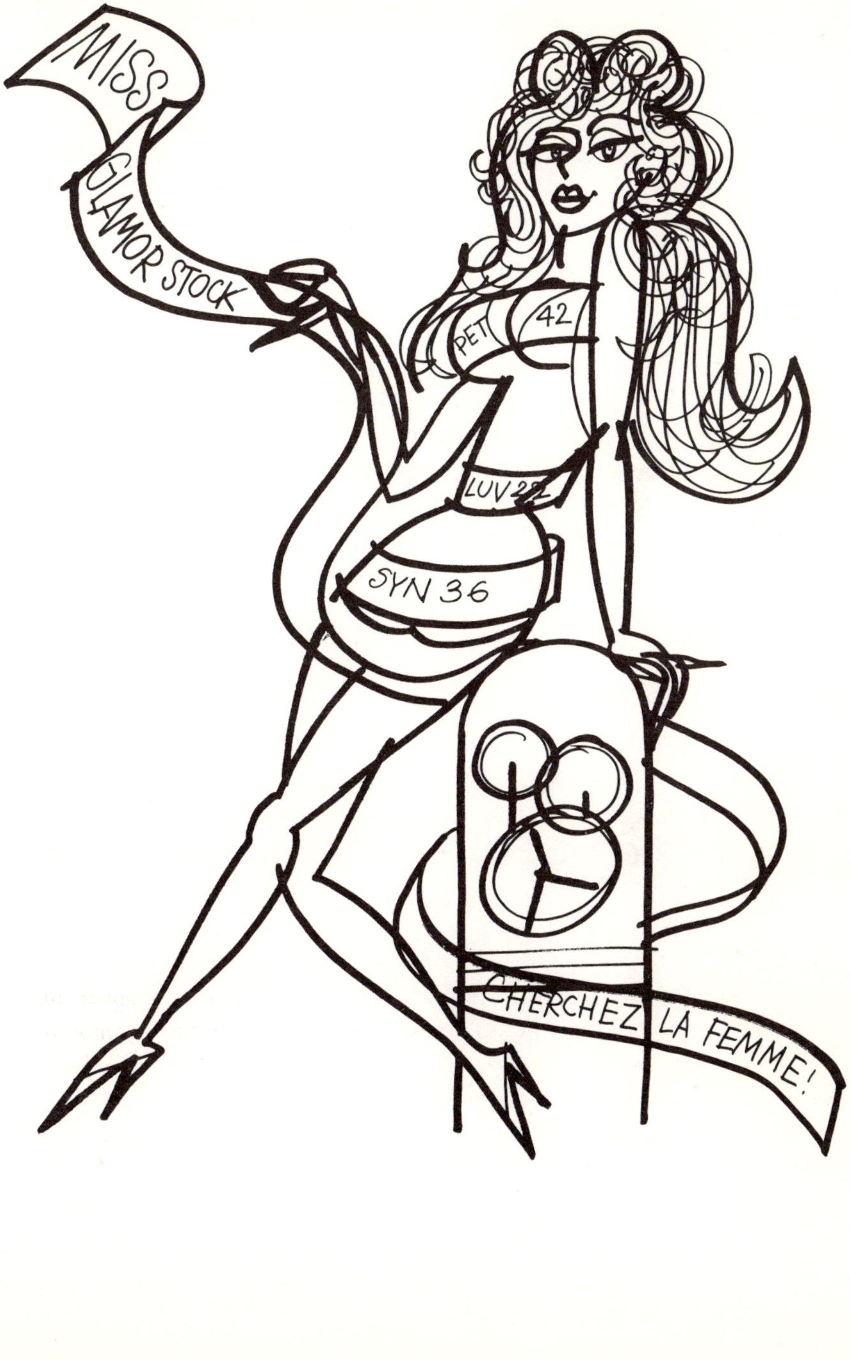
MISS
GLAMOR STOCK
PET 42
LUV 22
SYN 36
CHERCHEZ LA FEMME!

a little. He then eagerly makes a tour of the banquet circuit puffing up the stock and himself at the same time.

Brokerage houses and advisory services begin to recommend the stock. The stock becomes well known throughout the country and everyone begins talking about how high it will go. The first place it goes is on the Exchange, where the listing gives it respectability.

The stock becomes a trading favorite as it acquires a glamorous aura. The public is becoming infatuated and is rapidly falling in love. The homely dog changes into a glamor gal. Possessing an exotic name, she puts her best figures forward, splits as often as possible to be popular, and titilates across the tape luring her suitors like the sirens of ancient Greece. Upward, ever upward, she is courted, adored, and chased after. After years of careful preparation, a new star is born. . . .

> "If thou marriest a market shrew,
> Thou mayest not be able to tame her."
>
> Pop Singer

The Love Cycle of a Glamor Stock

ONCE INVESTORS look on a stock as a beautiful girl the cycle of love begins: inflation, love, marriage, and inevitably divorce. As in real life the more glamorous the girl the more she is sought after. And the more she is adored, the higher her price jumps. Occasionally, surrounded by many beaux, she often turns into a dog and bites the hand that once fed her.

On Wall Street the most popular stocks and those that have gone sky-high are called glamor stocks. It is nice to go after a beautiful girl, but she may prove difficult to live with. The most darling stocks have had many suitors. Remember the rapid rise of Thiokol, Brunswick, Transitron, and Universal Match? How they were courted by small investors, traders and mutual funds! But when these glamor gals grew a bit old, and their seductive beauty slowly began to fade, the most agile gigolos ran for the hills, leaving many broken hearts and empty hands.

The glamor stock is very similar to her human counterpart. She is vain, only caring for her looks, sometimes letting herself run down inside, while remaining beautiful outside. She is costly to buy, expensive to keep, and difficult to live with. Nevertheless, she always remains captivating and easy to fall in love with.

For every stock, there is a cycle of love. Farrington Corporation in the early 1960's went from 2 to 60 without ever earning a penny. Never have so many fallen in love with such a fickle woman. The losses widened each year and the stock dropped to 1½. At this point former terms of endearment turned into ungentlemanly slurs. The stock was soon considered a fallen woman, a dog, and something not to be touched with a ten-foot pole. Then, new management took over and restored the company's profitability. Suddenly, she became beautiful and entrancing again, as the stock rose to 55. Some of the same people who had thrown her out on the street came back begging for her favors. Six months later the stock dropped back to 1½. The cycle of glamorous infatuation, love, hate and despair had again come full circle.

The Hollywoodian distributor is well aware of the force that love exerts. Knowing this, what should you do when the right stock catches your eye? Selecting a stock is similar to dating. But when you are laying your money on the line, you are paying for the marriage license. What do you say when the broker leads you to the altar asking: "Do you take Miss Bobbie Brooks to be your lawfully wedded wife for better or for worse?"

Think!

(For better, yes; but do I want her for worse?)

(If she goes down in the morning, will I still love her in the afternoon?)

(Do I want to marry her or just live with her a while?)

Beware the miscarriage of marriage. You may like a

"I'm glad I only buy stocks I can sleep with."

stock and desire a permanent attachment. But it is better to treat a stock like a casual mistress, to be discarded after a pleasurable interlude.

When you have learned to "love 'em and leave 'em" then you may say . . .

"To the right—to the left—far and wide—with the shriek of a damned spirit! to my heart with the stealthy pace of the tiger! I alternately laughed and howled, as the one or the other idea grew predominant."

> Edgar Allan Poe, after having spent his first day in a brokerage house

Love on a Pendulum

For a better understanding of a market marriage, we must turn to another writer of the past—Edgar Allan Poe. He was an expert on pendulums and swingers. He was clearly ahead of his time, for he was the first to observe that playing the stock market is similar to riding a pendulum.

Edgar did so well as a creator of wild, fantastic tales that it was natural for him to switch to the stock market. After many violent swings, he finally flipped on his own pendulum and left this legacy to mankind:

The Pit and the Market Pendulum

Once upon a midnight dreary,
While I pondered weak and weary,
Much to my surprise
A vision of a pit
And a pendulum did arise.
And a fellow and a girl in love
Swung on the pendulum above.
To the left she was glad
While he was sad,

But to the right
What a happy sight!
Then as the pendulum soared,
Lightning crackled and storm clouds roared
Back and forth,
Maddened and gladdened
Through both wind and hail
Our forlorn friend did sail.
His strength sapped,
His mind snapped,
And quietly he let go
And fell into the pit below.
But while descending
He chanced to glance
At the pendulum ascending.
He to the depths did fall,
And she high above someone new did call.

    Everyone who plays the market finds himself on the pendulum of fortune and the girl is the stock of his dreams. Swinging to the right, he is riding a bull market where stocks are soaring and tipsters are roaring; veering to the left he is clinging to a bear market where stocks are falling and margin clerks are calling.

    When the pendulum of fortune swings his way, he is joyously triumphant, but when it turns, he becomes painfully despondent. As the trip gets rough and prices are falling, the pendulum sails faster and faster, and it becomes more and more difficult to hold on. When the swings become too violent and harrowing, the poor fellow is always ready to let go.

    Each stock has its own private pendulum waiting for each

buyer. It will test the investor's strength sooner or later. No stock has ever gone straight up, but rather swings back and forth. The pendulum is swayed by false rumors, international crises, bad newspaper reports and Dow Theory sell signals. Unfortunately, there usually comes a time when the pendulum has swung so far and the stock is dropping so fast that the rider can bear it no longer, and he lets go at the wrong time. While falling into the pit, he has enough time to look up and see his favorite stock soaring back up without him.

After a few moments, the forlorn fellow, both weak and weary, and sad and dreary, nostalgically looks up at the gal who jilted him and pleads longingly . . .

"Lover come back to me!"

"Paper profits are like dreamy clouds,
waiting to be blown away by the first Dow-Draft."
Old Proverb

Divorce – Wall Street Style

THE CYCLE of distribution and the circle of love have come full stream. The insiders have glamorized a stock, and sold her to the public. The outsiders have courted her and bid up the price for marrying her. This love story would have a happy ending except that the promoters are usually kicking their girl out of bed, just when the public is jumping into it.

The *distributors* have no difficulty in letting go, because they are not emotionally involved. They know she is showing signs of age, her figures are not as good as they used to be, and she is rapidly turning into a dog. The *distributees*, however, have fallen in love and they find it painful to leave a once faithful stock and all the little dividends. They fear that once they leave her, she may go places without them.

In market terms this translates into the overwhelming fear of selling a stock and seeing it go higher. Everyone claims that he is not looking for the high, but would settle for nothing less. Only God knows how high a stock will ultimately go, but He hasn't been talking to many people recently. Unfortunately, for investors' sake, the Heavenly

Edition of the *Wall Street Journal* hasn't been printed yet.

There is only one way to survive a market love affair. And that is to break the cycle before it breaks you. You may rely on your broker to help you realize when something is wrong. If he does not call you for several weeks, begin to worry. The longer you do not hear from him the more you have to worry about. When you finally call him and he gives you a nervous laugh, it is time to sweat a little. If you ask him for your quotes and he leaves out one stock, that is the one to worry about. When he finally admits it is down, he probably will say:

"Don't worry, nothing's changed but the price." (Which just happens to be everything.)

"The buying is smarter than the selling." (I wish I could have been as stupid as the sellers.)

"Just a lack of bids. It'll probably rally tomorrow." (If it does I'm running for the hills.)

These words of encouragement should definitely put you on your guard. However, if you should hear "It's time to average down"—*Run for your money*.

The difficulty here is that you may be getting out at the low. It would be better to formulate a new market principle which provides the grounds for divorce.

Treat each stock like a mistress.
If she performs well, stay with her.
But if she begins to falter, kick her out of bed
and get a new one.

"I never mind taking a profit. I always leave the other ten percent for the pigs."

3
The Distributors of New Issues

"The new issue market is just like duck hunting. Ninety-five percent of the ducks are shot down by five percent of the hunters."

Anonymous Duck

"The Midas Touch"

THE THIRD and perhaps the easiest method of distribution is through the new issue market. A new issue is a security that goes public, i.e., it is issued to the public for the first time. It is more like a glamorous debutante making her social debut, courted by scores of admiring beaux. Under such conditions her price often rises quickly, depending on the emotions aroused in her suitors. The success of a new issue depends on another human emotion—greed. Only greed can cause investors to chase after companies which have few assets but great hopes. Turning them into gold requires the talent of "The Midas Touch."

The reason it is the easiest form of distribution is that everyone wants part of the action. The number and type of companies is astounding—football and baseball players' fast-food franchises, movie stars' cosmetics, pet stores, and a wide assortment of dogs. Even the brokerage houses smell a good thing as even they yearn to go public. They have all realized the first important rule of new issues:

> *If you wish to make a fortune,*
> *don't buy anyone else's stock;*
> *have everyone else buy yours.*

If you buy stocks regularly, listed or unlisted, you may make 20% a year and occasionally double your money in several years. But if you are an insider of a company that initially sells its stock, you could conceivably make 1000% in a day. This is dynamic capitalism at its best wherein a group of *distributors* become instant millionaires.

The initial investors are very careful costwise, prudently spending pennies for stock that will go public for dollars. Although it may seem like sleight of hand the way a penny is quickly changed into a dollar, it can all be easily explained. The trick is to find someone to go public *to*. And, of course, the public is most obliging, for they feel that another benevolent soul will pay an even higher price an hour later.

Although a few solidly financed and highly profitable companies hit the new issue market, most are in need of money for "expansion or retirement of bank loans." Their accountants, also well versed in legerdemain, quote them the second underwriting principle:

> *In accordance with generally accepted*
> *accounting principles,*
> *when in dire financial condition,*
> *either declare bankruptcy or go public.*

It matters little whether the company is big or small or good or bad. During boiling markets the majority go up, buoyed along on hopes, dreams, and brokers making double the normal commission.

"THE MIDAS TOUCH"

Give an investor a glamorous name, a low price and a product he cannot understand and he will rush in confidently hoping for a 10-point rise. If it should drop $1/8$, he will rush out like a rabbit. Consequently, the investor continually seeks the hot issues, or those that will jump immediately, and tries to avoid the cold ones, which drop quickly.

The salesman, on the other hand, must sell all issues, receiving the ratio of 1000 cold shares to every 100 hot ones. As a result, there evolves a game. Customers are forever trying to hustle brokers out of the hot issues, while brokers are continually trying to hustle customers into the cold ones. It is thus frequently difficult to differentiate between the hustler and the hustlee.

The new issue market, which may thus be referred to as "The Big Hustle," becomes an irrational game. For the benefit of the public, here is the third and most practical principle of dealing with an underwriter:

*If you can get all you want of a new issue,
you don't want it;
if you can't get any, you want all you can get.*

If you cannot buy a hot issue, you should consider forming your own. Do you have the Midas Touch with other people's money? Here is your chance to become a distributor!

Suppose you have been a manure peddler all your life and decide to get class by becoming a fertilizer distributor. You incorporate the company and call yourself Natural Naturalizer. You work hard and peddle $200,000 worth of "naturalizer" a year and make $20,000 yearly. Nice, steady, reliable earnings. Then one day you notice that the firm you

HOW MANY SHARES OF AMALGAMATED FERTILIZER CAN YOU GET ME? I HEAR IT'S HOT.
MAN ARE YOU LUCKY! THE SALES MANAGER SAYS I CAN GET YOU ALL YOU WANT.
FORGET IT.

hired to computerize your bookkeeping has a swinging name: Compu-data-tronics. A business school graduate runs the company and rents a computer. The company has sales of $70,000 a year and manages to break even. But are the sales and future profits growing?! The fellow has a mathematics Ph.D. assistant who independently solves problems after creating them. That means research and development! You decide to merge with them and call it Naturized Computer Services and go public. Each partner will have 25,000 shares at 10 cents a share. The stock is split 10 for 1 and you decide to sell another 250,000 shares to the public at $5 a share, a nice low price. Of course, you now own 250,000 shares at one cent a share, also a nice low price.

You and your musketeers can't sell the stock locally, for your friends know you too well. You approach an underwriter, preferably a small one in another town, where you explain the company's operations and future plans:

"This company seems quite speculative," says one partner in the underwriting firm.

"I don't quite see the connection between fertilizer and computers," comments another.

"I wonder whether the public will buy such a package," asserts a third partner.

"We have a growing company. We're hiring more Ph.D's and we plan to have an 8% underwriting commission."

"I'm beginning to understand," replies the first partner. "It's a young conglomerate." (Translation: Each part of it's not worth a damn, but the whole conglomeration sounds pretty good.)

"We plan to issue a convertible bond after a year. And we'd like you to be on our board of directors."

"I see what you're driving at. You'll be a synergistic

amalgamation." (Translation: By energizing manure with computers we'll amalgamate fertilizer into gold.)

"We also plan to give the underwriter rights to buy 50,000 shares at one dollar."

"I think I got it. It's a concept stock." (Translation: I haven't the foggiest concept of what this company is all about.)

The stock comes out, the price opens at 7, and thus we have that miracle of miracles—that instant millionaire. The public is happy, they are ahead 40%. You, the business school graduate, and Ph.D problem solver, are ecstatic—with a 40,000% profit. And the underwriters are also delighted with their underwriting profits. All have finally found the best of all possible worlds.

Just so nobody sells.

4
The Lonely, Neurotic Distributor

"Sweet Are The Uses Of Their Adversity."
Jesse Livermore

The Short Seller
or
How to Lose Friends and Redistribute People

THE LONELIEST man on Wall Street is the short seller. He is the one who borrows a stock from a friend, sells it out, hopes it will drop so he can buy it back cheaper and return it, and then pockets the difference in profit. When he goes short he hopes that the friendly guy he borrowed the stock from loses his assets. Quite naturally, he is also short of friends.

The short seller is extremely unpopular, simply because he is publicly recognized as a dedicated *distributor*. For decades he has had a bad image and could use a public relations uplift. In past eras he has been accused of causing major declines as well as hoping for them. Despite the hostility of the crowd, he still stands up to be counted—especially once a month when the short interest figures are reported.

Under the pressure, he is known to become paranoiac, feeling that everyone is after him. He continually feels persecuted as government officials have an occasion tried to banish him entirely from the market. When traders learn that there are many shorts in the same stock they purposely plunge in to force the price up and scare the shorts out of their pants.

The short becomes neurotically fearful of crowds. When he learns there are a hundred thousand other shorts with him in a stock he often panics for the exit, which becomes a painful squeeze as everyone gets the same idea. He fears that when the stock rises and he begins to lose money, that stock may rise from here to infinity.

He acquires a psychotic sense of humor. He smiles during every market decline, grins when glamor stocks plunge, and howls with leg-slapping laughter when a company goes bankrupt.

So, this lonely, neurotic *distributor* plods on. With all his ills there is one overriding fear: that someday he may suddenly wake up and find himself a *distributee*. This is a terrifying thought and is the source of all his neuroses. He can face anything but the idea of becoming a distributed *distributor*.

The short seller may thus be considered the bravest of the *distributors*. Though bereft of friends, pursued by vulturous traders, and rattled by upticks, he bravely bares the ills of others. He knows the dangers of his position, but finds security in the knowledge passed down through the ages:

"Sweet are the uses of adversity—if it is not thy own."

Four

THE POWER BEHIND WALL STREET

Who Are "They"?

NO MATTER who or what you are in the market, somewhere in your career you must have heard, "They are buying." And if they were, could you have been far behind? Although they prefer to remain behind the scenes, their impact on the market is always great. The mere mention of their name sometimes causes the ticker tape to palpitate.

Who are "they"? The crowd. Everyone wants to know about the crowd and how they operate. Although their names are secret, here is an unauthorized description of some of its members.

"Their Crowd"

ONE OF the sneakiest words in Wall Street jargon is "they." This vague pronoun is used to describe a secret group of omniscient seers who oversee the market. "They" are always selling before the crash. "They" are making out with all the broads. But who *are* "they"? Nobody knows, for "they" are always crouching under quotation marks.

Every major field has its "they's," and no matter where one may go, or what stock one buys, one will usually find a "they" there first. And neither you nor I nor we can do anything about it, for the "they's" have it. The identity of the individuals in this mysterious society will unfortunately never be fully known, for there is no such thing as a *Who's They* of finance.

"Theyism" is not a modern happening. In ancient times it was "Thou" that had all the answers, especially in the Ten Commandments. Somewhere between "thou" and "thee" and "thine," "they" secretly took over. Can an ordinary person become a member of the group? It is doubtful, unless you have connections, are born therein, or marry a "theiress."

When you enter the stock market, you are welcome to join the public, but you are never invited into the Wall Street clan which has the power to move stocks. "Their Crowd" is a money crowd. They represent the only power that counts—big money. Their influence is great and far reaching. When they decree that it is time to move out—get out of their way or you will be flattened. Big money is power and the crowd is governed only by their own

GOLDEN RULE
*Those who have the gold
make all the rules.*

There are the insiders who know everything, long before the outsiders know anything. The insiders are usually buying your stock at the bottom of the pit and selling it back to you at the top of the pendulum.

Mutual funds are some of the biggest "they's" of Wall Street. When they move into a stock, the tape is painted with a barrage of block trades, and their very action causes the rise in the stock. Traders, sharpies, fast-buck artists and other financial parasites hop on the soaring star, only to find it turn into a fallen angel when the funds move out.

There is also a group known as the "smart money." They are considered smart because they only buy absolute winners. It is most evident in the new issue market, where the original investors exchange their paper for gold. It is the only time in history that the "they's" must reveal their names, for it is required by law towards the back of the new issue prospectus. They don't mind, for it's kind of nice to show off how smart they really are.

The analysts also carry great weight in the market. They love to shoot down high-flying stocks, for they are jealous

"Don't look now, but there go a couple of 'Theys.'"

of people who can make money in the market. They are known to the public as Security Analysts, and to the crowd as Security Annihilators. It is difficult to make a name for themselves by praising companies; it is far easier to be positively negative and look smart when the stocks go down the next day because of the panic their bad reports have created. One was heard to whisper, "I never met a stock I couldn't hate."

These *their*ian forms do not encourage converts, and prefer to remain a secret clan. You, we, it, whatever thou be, must realize by now that the "they's" want you to stay in your bowl. The only thing the crowd does not want is that you should ever realize that:

> *They*
>   cannot succeed without
>   *You.*

Five

ADAM SMITH'S MODEL OF THE SYSTEM

"And it must follow, as the night the day."
William Shakespeare

The Distribution Cycle

ADAM SMITH, like the economists who followed him, was always asking questions, searching for the true nature of things. Where does the money come from and where does it go? Why are there so few rich and so many poor? Why should Howard Hughes make $200 million a year and security analysts $200 a week?

To arrive at some answers Adam began to construct the first "economic models," drawing lines, curves and circles, hoping they would intersect somewhere before they went off the page. Fortunately they met, and from that point on economists have been forever going in circles.

Every economic system must be graphically portrayed so that ordinary people can easily grasp its basic principles. The distribution system can be clarified by picturing it as flowing along a cyclical movement. We can then show how each element in the system functions and contributes to the whole.

The cycle may be best understood by portraying it in the manner of a classical economic model. Just as every stock has its highs and lows for the year, so does the model on the next page portray the ups and downs of the redistribution theory:

The cycle is composed of two circular lines, following a parallel movement. The inner one represents the insider or *distributor* who accumulates stocks at low prices, stirs up enthusiasm as they rise, distributes them at high prices, and then re-accumulates them again at the bottom of the cycle. The outer line portrays the outsider or *distributee* who is emotionally aroused to buy into the distribution area, only to become gradually disenchanted and sell out at the troughs of the cycle.

Throughout the movement both members are always acting opposite the other, one always buying when the other is selling. The *distributor* may be considered a sadist who enjoys inflicting pain on others. The *distributee* is closer to a masochist who enjoys taking the regular beatings. Together they form the perfect market marriage.

Their interlocking relationship is the basis of the cyclical stock market. Economists regard a cycle as movements around a fixed position. There must also be a force that brings these fluctuations back to the originating point. Translating this to English, what goes up must come down whether it be an apple or a stock. And there must be some force besides gravity causing the movement.

In our theoretical model the force is human emotions. Some strong feeling, whether it be love or hate or greed compels "irrational man" to chase after rising stocks, while fear or despair makes him flee stocks at their lows. Such emotions are the impetus for the continuous market cycle.

We have seen these emotional forces in action—the hatred of the crowd helping Howard Hughes redistribute Wall Street, the glamorous love affair enabling the Holly-

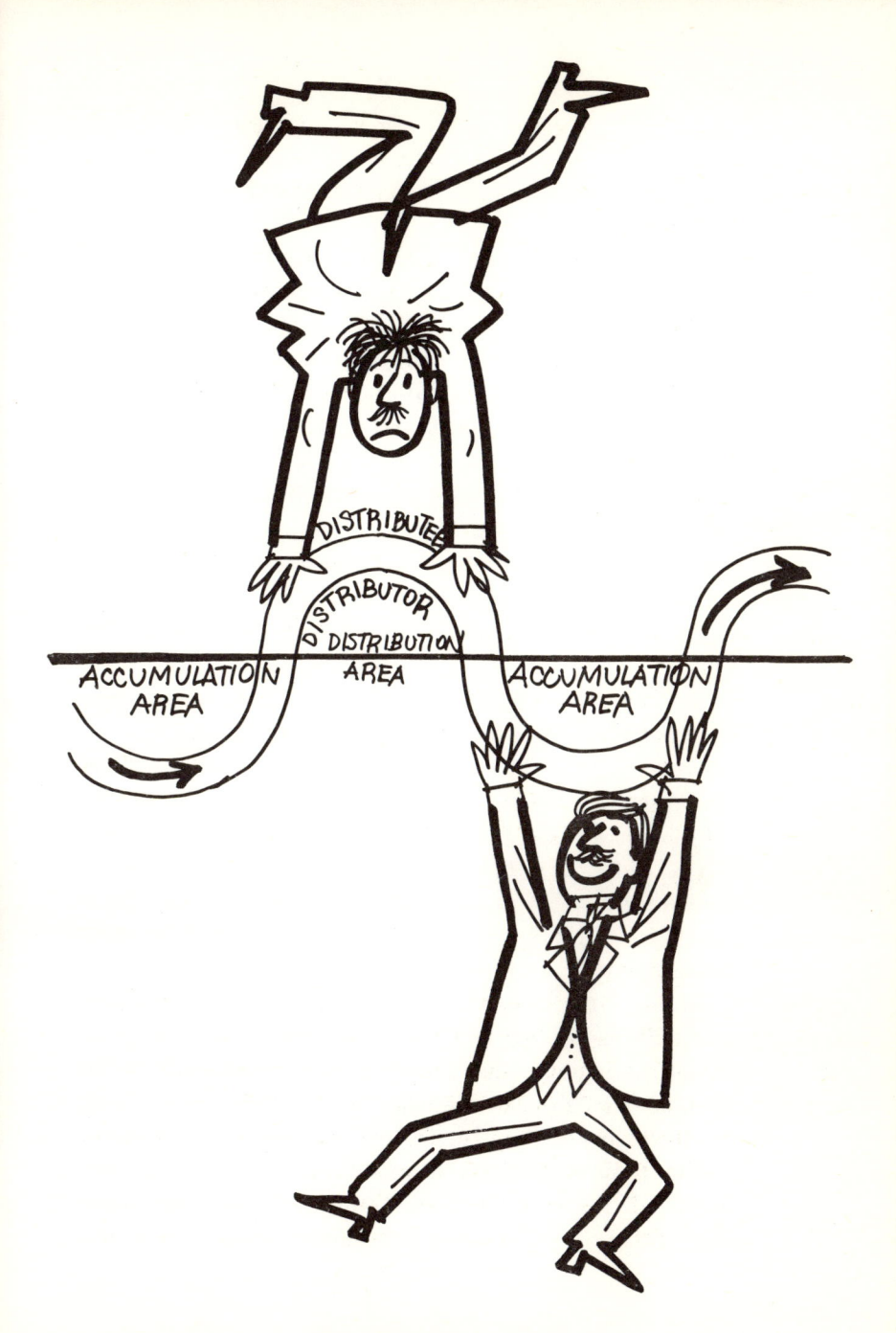

The Distribution Cycle

woodian mogul to score, and the greed of the public chasing new issues.

It is important to realize that there is nothing permanent about the *distributor-distributee* relationship. This year's *distributor* can become next year's *distributee,* and vice-versa. This is due to the freedom of opportunity inherent in the market—the freedom to rise above one's class.

The stock market, like the real world it reflects, has its own class distinctions, with those at the highest distributorial level always striving to retain their identity while the lower levels are always trying to change theirs.

The distribution cycle may also be pictured as a wheel with the different market groups on different levels forming a hierarchy.

As can be seen, the lowly *distributees* have a long way to go to get to the top. If they had to depend on their own abilities to get there, it would indeed be hopeless for the majority. But the real hope for them lies in the nature of the system itself—its own self-equalizing mechanism.

This process has come to be known as the Earthquake Effect, which is a financial cataclysm, occurring once a decade on Wall Street. When the quake strikes, everyone's capital gets shifted, some *distributors* becoming *distributees* and some "they's" turning into "we's." Such tremors have occurred in '29, '38, '46, '57, '62 and '70, each quake resulting in a general redistribution of wealth.

The Distributorial Hierarchy fears the Earthquake Effect for they know they are in danger. When the crevices open up, the stocks plunge before there has been time to efficiently distribute them. With these tremulous eruptions, the wheel can be shaken so it looks like the illustration on page 124.

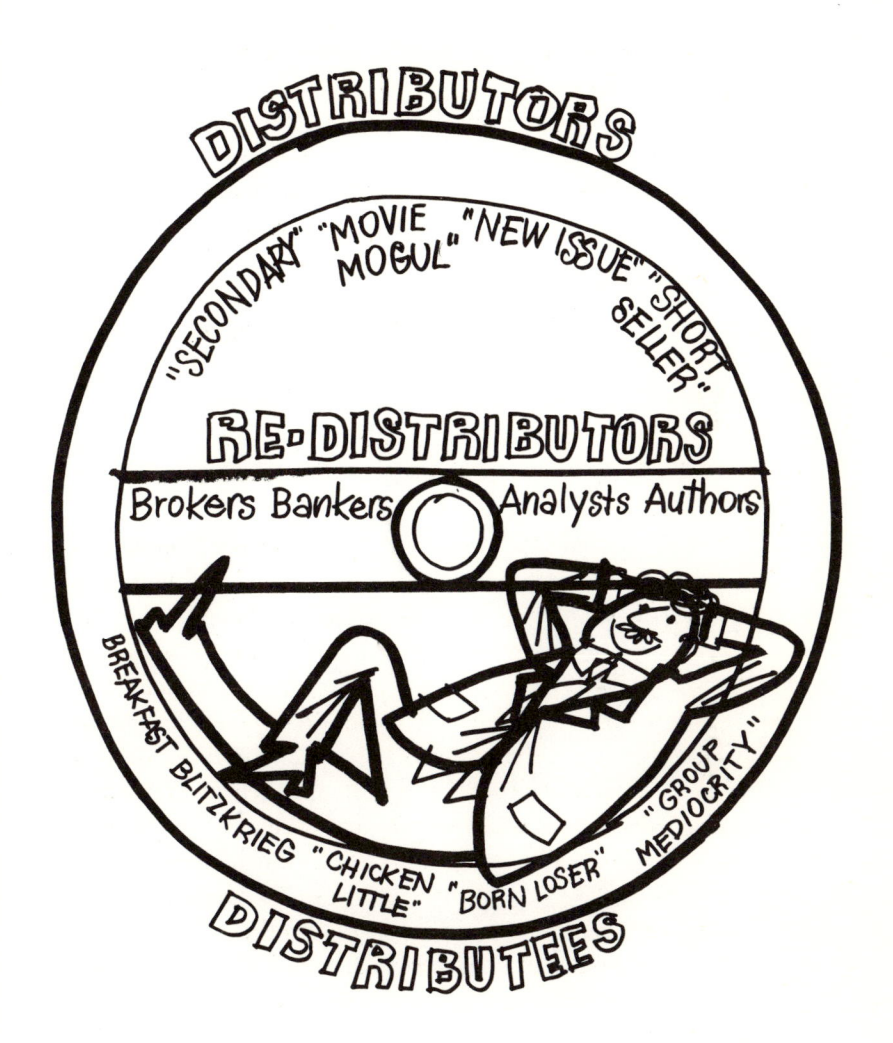

Distribution Wheel

DISTRIBUTEES
"GROUP MEDIOCRITY"
"BORN LOSER"
"LITTLE CHICKEN"
"BREAKFAST BLITZKRIEG"
Brokers, Bankers
Specialists
Analysts, Authors
Underwriters
RE-DISTRIBUTORS
"SECONDARY"
"MOVIE MOGUL"
"NEW ISSUE"
"SHORT SELLER"
DISTRIBUTORS

THE DISTRIBUTION CYCLE

Three results of this effect should be noted:

The first is the way *distributors* are sometimes jolted out of their high levels and plunge straight down, often never to return. This can be seen in the careers of some of the great market heros of the past such as Will Durant, Robert R. Young, and Jesse Livermore. All fell off their pendulums and soon discovered they had much further to drop than ordinary mortals. They also found the idea of becoming an ordinary *distributee* so revolting that they eventually shot themselves. Others could swear it was like falling off a skyscraper, only they weren't dreaming. Such is the precarious nature of a *distributor* when the market gets shaken up.

The second is the rotating of some *distributees* to the top. Many will not know how to handle their newly found wealth and will eventually slip back down. Others will probably stay on top for another decade.

Third and most important is the steadfastness of the *redistributors*, who in spite of the upheavals, remain unshaken, fixed in their position. They are the middlemen of the market, helping it flow along for a fee but skillfully avoiding being engulfed themselves. Therefore, they stay out of the market, untouchable and undistributable.

This latter group bears closer scrutiny, for they evidently know something that the general public is unaware of. There is something that keeps them from playing the market. Let us try to discover why they, like the angels, fear to trade.

Six

THE LEGACY
OF ADAM SMITH

"The only thing money can't buy is poverty."
John Paul Getty

How You May Become a Beneficiary

ALTHOUGH YOU may find the principles of this book enlightening, you may still ask "How do I make money?" After all, making money is the only excuse for playing the market. You may also ask what chance have you got when even economists have trouble making money. You do have a chance if you learn the secret of becoming a beneficiary of the market.

Let us return to Adam Smith and see if we may benefit from his experiences. You will recall that Adam entered the market because he believed that it was a rational system operating under the established rules of logic. Adam was a brilliant thinker, but he miscalculated when he concluded that he could beat the market by actually playing it. He thought he could apply his normal, everyday reasoning to the logic of the market. But the market does not seem to follow the rules of common sense. If a person receives a raise, he is worth more. If the company raises the dividend, the stock drops. If a person strikes oil, his net worth goes up. If the oil companies are awarded Alaskan oil leases, their stocks plunge. Rational conclusion:

What is logical for your personal life is illogical for the market.

This is the legacy of Adam Smith who discovered that the stock market is an irrational system founded on the principles of disorder, confusion, and chaos. Fear, greed, and hysteria clearly dominate over reason. The market ebbs and flows with the alternating moods of investor euphoria and depression which in turn sweep away all reason.

Stock prices continually move in either direction, but the cogent reasons, as dutifully reported in the daily newspapers, are not the cause of the fluctuations. Prices rise and fall first—then comes the alleged reason for the move, and the public simply follows afterwards and reinforces the trend. When prices rise, all bad news is filtered out and good news gradually emerges. When stocks start dropping, the good news is filtered out and the bad news takes over. The logical cause-and-effect relationships of the real world are reversed in the illogic of the stock market.

Although prices are volatile, reasons are flexible. If the market should soar, the General Motors strike is considered a stimulant to the market, helping to cool the inflationary forces and lower interest rates. But when prices begin to drop, the strike is viewed as a depressant to the economy boosting the unemployment rate and raising fears of a recession. This flexibility thus allows any reason to follow stocks up or down.

Prices, then, have little to do with the company they represent. Many bad companies sell at very high prices and some good ones are discounted very cheaply. Neither has anything to do with "value."

We may also conclude that the average person cannot cope with such a system. His emotions betray his reason and this is why he loses. He can only buy stocks when he feels good, and he feels good most of the time when stocks are high. On the reverse side he will only sell stocks when he feels bad which is most often when prices are low. How he feels when he wakes up in the morning is probably more important than any analysis of companies and earnings projections. His daily moods, therefore, are his rationale for playing the market.

What can the reasonable people do? They and you can join the group we have not yet discussed—the *beneficiaries*. These are the people who consistently benefit from the operation of the market. Although you may think that the *distributors* are the main beneficiaries of the market, experience has shown that they lack stability. Once or twice a decade they trip and fall into a crevice, giving back all they have accumulated on the way up. To be sure, some like Bernard Baruch and Joseph Kennedy survived all calamities, but they are the exceptions. The *distributors* are simply too erratic to be the consistent beneficiaries of the system.

The real beneficiaries are the *redistributors* of wealth, helping others to redistribute their wealth while slowly accumulating and keeping theirs. They are the pillars of the market, steadfast through all periods. They are the only ones who consistently benefit from the market cycle, always keeping their heads, while others may be losing theirs. They have discovered that the secret of beating the system is to go around it, on it, under it, but never in it. They have evolved their own guiding principle:

The most rational way
to make a fortune in the market,
is not to play it.

And so they have withdrawn, preferring to make their money off the market, rather than in it. Of course some have to play the market due to the nature of their jobs—the specialists, over-the-counter traders, and underwriters. But they are very careful not to hold any stock very long, operating under the "hot potato" syndrome. They are very quick to hand it off before ever getting burned. At the same time they are wise enough not to publicize their market *operandi*. The *beneficiaries* will never admit who or what they are, but insist they are helping you and the economy of the nation:

The stock exchanges exhort you to buy a share in the future of America, but they never own any stock.

The bankers will gladly supply you with capital to play the market, but would rather call a loan than own a stock.

The advisory services and security analysts are delighted to recommend possible winners, but prefer not to take their own advice.

The brokers love to sell secondary distributions, but do not want to get stuck with any themselves.

And the stock market writers are dedicated to writing *How To Make a Million* books which are only rewarding to their authors.

The *beneficiaries* are then seen to be the epitome of "Rational Man." They understand the system and have learned how to live outside it, indirectly benefitting from it.

The *distributee* must also learn to adjust. Only the "rational men" earn a steady living through the market, because they do not play it. The little guy is characterized as irrational because he does play it. He can receive no benefit outside the market. He is condemned to the endless march of the ticker tape. To win, he must somehow transform himself into "Rational Man," but unfortunately he runs into the stock market *"Catch-22a"* which states that any rational person who plays the market ought to have his head examined.

Regardless of your mental condition there are several options open to you in or out of the market:

You may decide to buck the odds and continue to play the market in your normal way, hoping that the "earthquake effect" will shift you from a loser to a winner. But this requires too much luck and great patience to rely on such a windfall.

You may also try to play the role of a *distributor*. Unfortunately this usually requires big power and big money. And being a little guy does put you at a great disadvantage. If you insist, however, your best chance is as a *new issue distributor*, which is highly regarded as a means to instant wealth. You must have a talent for shrewdness, putting up a minimum of capital and issuing a maximum of shares. The advantage here is that if you are shrewd enough you do not really "play" the market; you have the public "play" it for you. Success will depend on your ability to form a private company at low, low prices and through promotion hope that the public will take it up, up and away.

Your last alternative is the most practical. It does not take much talent or money; you may even be mediocre, which could help. Try to become a *beneficiary* of the system, indirectly of course.

Either become:
 A broker
 A security analyst
 A vice-president at a bank
 Or, an author,

Or, better yet, take advantage of the accumulated wisdom of this book and
>Start an Advisory Service.

Seven

THE FUTURE OF THE MARKET

> "Not with a bang but a whimper."
> T. S. Eliot

Can the Cycle End?

ASKING WHETHER the market could ever stop going up or down may seem as foolish as asking whether the buttonwood tree could come unbuttoned or whether brokers could go broke. On the surface—nonsense—but underneath, quite sensible. In an irrational system all things are possible. And who is to say that money will flow forever out of one wallet and into another?

There could come a day when the cycle may not recycle. Of course no one is planning on this. Brokerage houses have been busily opening up new offices and computerizing operations faster than stocks have been falling. They are gearing themselves for the expected huge volume of the '70's and 80's. The Dow Jones average is being projected at anywhere from 1000 to 2001 in the future. In short, the whole financial community is reaching for a financial moon, but may wind up with sixpence.

There are dark clouds on the horizon. The brokerage houses are having trouble making a profit regardless of market conditions. In a bull market the volume is too high for them to handle so they close one day a week. In bear markets the volume is too low, so some are closing seven days a week.

Some analysts are worried about the price of gold rising, the dollar being devalued and the market going lower. The economy is cooling off, unemployment is rising, retail sales are lagging, but no one will admit there is a recession. Companies are illiquid, everyone wanting to borrow in the bond markets. So many people have bought high-yielding bonds that there is not much money left for the stock market.

A healthy market is crucial to the nation's welfare. More and more people now depend on the market for their income. The analysts recommend the stocks, the brokers sell them. The newspapers keep their circulation up by carrying the final prices. Even the government is supported by the taxes of the winners.

With the market assuming such an important role in our society, there is naturally great concern over its future. The experts, however, are worrying over the wrong things. The economy will rebound, the dollar will prevail, and the companies will survive the downturn. But the market will not necessarily go on forever. It may be doomed for internal reasons.

The 1970 market crash has pointed up the inherent weakness of the system: Some of its members are unstable. The recent "earthquake effect" has unsettled an entire generation of investors, and in its course shaken up the whole market.

Many of our most noted "rational" *redistributors*—the brokers, advisory services and bankers—have been caught acting "irrationally." They have made the inexcusable error of taking their own advice in the market. Nothing else can explain why so many are on the verge of bankruptcy.

CAN THE CYCLE END?

At the same time a large number of formerly reliable *distributors*—entrepreneurial conglomerate promoters, mutual fund managers, and venture capitalists—have unwittingly decimated each other.

But the major concern rests with the *distributee*, the "irrational" little guy who has been so important in the past. Silently and slowly he has begun changing his spots. He is no longer rushing in to buy, and is thus impeding the movement and accumulation of wealth. The market could very well be in grave danger. Just as in the cycles of nature, if one key element of a system should disappear there can be dire consequences for the rest. In the stock market an important element is also disappearing: *The little guy is leaving the market.*

He is irritated by higher commissions and tired of losing. He is peeved at brokers ignoring him because his orders are small. Piqued by the indifference of the system, he has begun to withdraw. There can be only one explanation for this change in his thinking: The irrational little man is becoming rational.

Imagine what could happen without him: Young companies could not go public, for there would be no one to go go public *to;* secondary distributions could not be sold, for there would be no one to distribute to; the *distributors* would have to distribute to each other. This is where the system is breaking down. There must be someone to sell stocks to at the highs. But here is the rub. The small investor never minded being redistributed, for he has always been a dedicated masochist. The big money interests, however, find the idea of redistributing themselves revolting and un-American. The mutual funds and large traders would rebel and leave the scene. Ultimately we could return to the lazy ticker tape days of the 30's, where each trade was greeted with a cheer and the brokers were playing with each other.

Aware of this possibility, the beneficiaries are eager to see it speed up again. But the little guy refuses to cooperate. The desperate *distributors* are searching for any buyer who may be caught breathing on the tape, but the new "rational man" is running off the tape.

As a result the market is beginning to buckle under the strain. Cracked by severe financial quakes and crashing stocks, the high-speed ticker tape is gradually decelerating, slowly grinding to an inevitable halt. And one fine morning, gleaming neon letters will proclaim the coming market cataclysm which will end not with a whimper, but with an apocalyptic bang.

Have we painted an exaggerated picture of the future? Will these dire predictions come to pass or can something still be done to save the system? Yes, there is hope. The market's future rests on the shoulder of the little guy. The question is: Can he be enticed back on the ticker tape? Not through cajolery, but perhaps a call to a deep feeling of patriotism could help stir up his juices.

An advertisement could appear in the *Wall Street Journal:*

PROLETARIAT OF THE MARKET
UNITE!

You have the right to remain in the market cycle. Not only that, but you have the responsibility to save the system. Capitalism cannot survive without you. Adam Smith recognized the freedom of each individual to do his own thing. The constitution guarantees you certain freedoms—to speak, to write, to act. No matter how difficult the struggle may seem, you must go on.

Earthquake Effect

You have the inalienable rights to life, liberty and the pursuit of losing your ass.

So take heart like a soldier going into battle. Hold your head up high, with your sword boldly out front and think of those stirring lines in Shakespeare's *Henry V* as the King exhorts his troops to action:

> When the blast of war blows in your ears,
> Then imitate the action of the tiger;
> Stiffen the sinews, summon up the blood,
> Disguise fair nature with hard-favour'd rage
> And once more, dear friends . . .

Unto the breach!

Appendix

THE TEN COMMANDMENTS OF A BROKER

I. Thou shalt not lie, but never admit the truth.

II. Thou shalt promise the moon, but deliver at least sixpence.

III. Thou shalt buy, buy, buy, and sell, sell, sell, just so it is not thy own money.

IV. Thou shalt not covet thy competitor's customers; simply beg, borrow or steal them.

V. Thou shalt always see light at the end of the tunnel even if it be nighttime, and even if there be no tunnel.

VI. Thou shalt always protect thyself, and if there is any time left over, do thy job.

VII. Honor thy wealthy clients and thy mutual funds with hot new issues.

VIII. Thou shalt be a bold bull or a fearless bear with thy customer's money, while always banking thy own money.

IX. Thou shalt always keep the money flowing so fast that thy customers know not what they do, nor what they own.

X. Thou shalt not commit—thyself.